Cram101 Textbook Outlines to accompany:

Business Marketing: Connecting Strategy, Relationships, and Learning

Dwyer & Tanner, 4th Edition

A Cram101 Inc. publication (c) 2009.

PRACTICE EXAMS.

Get all of the self-teaching practice exams for each chapter of this textbook at **www.Cram101.com** and ace the tests. Here is an example:

Chapter 1

Business Marketing: Connecting Strategy, Relationships, and Learning
Dwyer & Tanner, 4th Edition,
All Material Written and Prepared by Cram101

I WANT A BETTER GRADE.   Items 1 - 50 of 100.

1 _____ AG is a German chemical company and the largest chemical company in the world. _____ has customers in over 200 countries and supplies products to a wide variety of industries. Despite its size and global presence _____ receives little public attention as it has abandoned consumer product lines in the 90s.

○ BASF   ○ B.C.G. analysis
○ B2B marketplace   ○ Baby busters

2 _____ is the practice of organizations, including commercial businesses, governments and institutions, facilitating the sale of their products or services to other companies or organizations that in turn resell them, use them as components in products or services they offer, or use them to support their operations.

○ Business marketing   ○ B.C.G. analysis
○ B2B marketplace   ○ Baby busters

3 _____ was a company whose direct predecessor was established in the USA by Charles William Post as the Postum Cereal Company. C.W. Post was an astute businessman who believed that advertizing and aggressive marketing were the keys to a successful enterprise. _____ was acquired by Philip Morris Companies for $5.6 billion, the largest non-oil acquisition to that time.

○ General Foods   ○ G.E. multi factoral analysis
○ Gadzooks   ○ GAF Corporation

4 _____ is a United States company specializing in the production of salt for food, water conditioning, industrial, agricultural, and road/highway use.

You get a 50% discount for the online exams. Go to **Cram101.com**, click Sign Up at the top of the screen, and enter DK73DW4509 in the promo code box on the registration screen. Access to Cram101.com is $4.95 per month, cancel at any time.

With Cram101.com online, you also have access to extensive reference material.

You will nail those essays and papers. Here is an example from a Cram101 Biology text:

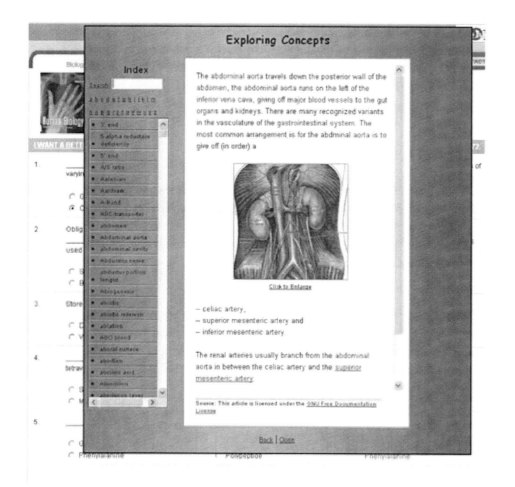

Learning System

Cram101 Textbook Outlines is a learning system. The notes in this book are the highlights of your textbook, you will never have to highlight a book again.

How to use this book. Take this book to class, it is your notebook for the lecture. The notes and highlights on the left hand side of the pages follow the outline and order of the textbook. All you have to do is follow along while your instructor presents the lecture. Circle the items emphasized in class and add other important information on the right side. With Cram101 Textbook Outlines you'll spend less time writing and more time listening. Learning becomes more efficient.

Cram101.com Online

Increase your studying efficiency by using Cram101.com's practice tests and online reference material. It is the perfect complement to Cram101 Textbook Outlines. Use self-teaching matching tests or simulate in-class testing with comprehensive multiple choice tests, or simply use Cram's true and false tests for quick review. Cram101.com even allows you to enter your in-class notes for an integrated studying format combining the textbook notes with your class notes.

Visit **www.Cram101.com**, click Sign Up at the top of the screen, and enter **DK73DW4509** in the promo code box on the registration screen. Access to www.Cram101.com is normally $9.95, but because you have purchased this book, your access fee is only $4.95. Sign up and stop highlighting textbooks forever.

Business Marketing: Connecting Strategy, Relationships, and Learning
Dwyer & Tanner, 4th

CONTENTS

1. Introduction to Business Marketing 2
2. The Character of Business Marketing 14
3. The Purchasing Function 28
4. Organizational Buyer Behavior 42
5. Market Opportunities: Current and Potential Customers 50
6. Marketing Strategy 60
7. Weaving Marketing into the Fabric of the Firm 76
8. Developing and Managing Offerings: What Do Customers Want? 84
9. Business Marketing Channels: Partnerships for Customer Service 98
10. Creating Customer Dialogue 110
11. Communicating via Advertising, Trade Shows, and PR 120
12. The One-to-One Media 134
13. Sales and Sales Management 142
14. Pricing and Negotiating for Value 154
15. Evaluating Marketing Efforts 166
16. Customer Retention and Maximization 176

BASF	BASF AG is a German chemical company and the largest chemical company in the world. BASF has customers in over 200 countries and supplies products to a wide variety of industries. Despite its size and global presence BASF receives little public attention as it has abandoned consumer product lines in the 90s.
Business marketing	Business marketing is the practice of organizations, including commercial businesses, governments and institutions, facilitating the sale of their products or services to other companies or organizations that in turn resell them, use them as components in products or services they offer, or use them to support their operations.
General Foods	General Foods was a company whose direct predecessor was established in the USA by Charles William Post as the Postum Cereal Company. C.W. Post was an astute businessman who believed that advertizing and aggressive marketing were the keys to a successful enterprise. General Foods was acquired by Philip Morris Companies for $5.6 billion, the largest non-oil acquisition to that time.
Morton Salt	Morton Salt is a United States company specializing in the production of salt for food, water conditioning, industrial, agricultural, and road/highway use.
Marketing	Marketing is the process or act of bringing together buyers and sellers. Two major factors of marketing are the recruitment of new customers and the retention and expansion of relationships with existing customers. Marketing methods are informed by many of the social sciences, particularly psychology, sociology, and economics.
Consumer	Consumer refers to individuals or households that purchase and use goods and services generated within the economy.
Consumer behavior	Consumer behavior is the study of how people buy, what they buy, when they buy and why they buy. It blends elements from psychology, sociology, sociopsychology, anthropology and economics. It attempts to understand the buyer decision making process, both individually and in groups. It studies characteristics of individual consumers such as demographics, psychographics, and behavioral variables in an attempt to understand people's wants. It also tries to assess influences on the consumer from groups such as family, friends, reference groups, and society in general.
Career	Career is a term defined as the course or progress through life.
Distribution	Distribution is one of the 4 aspects of marketing. Traditionally, distribution has been seen as dealing with logistics: how to get the product or service to the customer. There have also been some innovations in the distribution of services. For example, there has been an increase in franchizing and in rental services - the latter offering anything from televisions through tools.
Distribution channel	Frequently there may be a chain of intermediaries, each passing the product down the chain to the next organization, before it finally reaches the consumer or end-user. This process is known as the distribution channel.
Sales	Sales is the act of providing a product or service in return for money or other compensation. It is an act of completion of a commercial activity.
Corporation	A corporation is a legal entity which has a separate legal personality from its members. The defining legal rights and obligations of the corporation are: the ability to sue and be sued; the ability to hold assets in its own name; the ability to hire agents; the ability to sign contracts; and the ability to make by-laws, which govern its internal affairs.
Dell	Dell develops, manufactures, sells and supports personal computers, servers, data storage devices, network switches, personal digital assistants, software, televisions, computer peripherals and other technology-related products.
Integration	Economic integration refers to reducing barriers among countries to transactions and to movements of goods, capital, and labor, including harmonization of laws, regulations, and standards. Integrated markets theoretically function as a unified market.

Go to **Cram101.com** for the Practice Tests for this Chapter.

Strategy	A strategy is a long term plan of action designed to achieve a particular goal, most often "winning". Strategy is differentiated from tactics or immediate actions with resources at hand by its nature of being extensively premeditated, and often practically rehearsed.
DuPont	DuPont is an American chemical company that is currently the world's second largest chemical company in terms of market capitalization and fourth in revenue.
Du Pont family	The Du Pont family is an American family descended from Pierre Samuel du Pont de Nemours. The son of a Paris watchmaker and a member of a Burgundian noble family, he and his sons, Victor Marie du Pont and Eleuthère Irénée du Pont, emigrated to the United States in 1800 and used the resources of this heritage to found one of the most prominent of American families, and one of its most successful corporations, E. I. du Pont de Nemours and Company,
Marketing research	Marketing Research is a form of business research and is generally divided into two categories: consumer market research and business-to-business market research, which was previously known as Industrial Marketing Research.
Market	A market is, as defined in economics, a social arrangement that allows buyers and sellers to discover information and carry out a voluntary exchange of goods or services.
Research	Research is a human activity based on intellectual investigation and aimed at discovering, interpreting, and revising human knowledge on different aspects of the world. Research can use the scientific method, but need not do so.
Boise Cascade Holdings, LLC	Boise Cascade Holdings, LLC, which uses the trade name Boise, is an American pulp and paper company, ranked as the thirteenth largest forest products company in the world.
Government	A government is "the organization that is the governing authority of a political unit," "the ruling power in a political society," and the apparatus through which a governing body functions and exercises authority.
Government agency	A government agency is a permanent or semi-permanent organization in the machinery of government that is responsible for the oversight and administration of specific functions, such as an intelligence agency.
Original equipment manufacturer	Original equipment manufacturer, refers to a situation in which one company purchases a manufactured product from another company and resells the product as its own, usually as a part of a larger product it sells. It is the company that originally manufactured the product.
Users	Users refer to people in the organization who actually use the product or service purchased by the buying center.
Customer	Customer is someone who makes use of or receives the products or services of an individual or organization.
Manufacturing	Manufacturing is the use of tools and labor to make things for use or sale. The term may refer to a vast range of human activity, from handicraft to high tech, but is most commonly applied to industrial production, in which raw materials are transformed into finished goods on a large scale.
C. M. Tanner Wholesale Grocery	C. M. Tanner Wholesale Grocery is a company that wholesales general line groceries, hardware food planning services, food security services, food reserves management, surplus management, food and nutrition policy planning and programs, and hunger eradication programs. The company is located in Carrollton, Georgia.
Hotel	A hotel is an establishment that provides paid lodging, usually on a short-term basis. It often provides a number of additional guest services such as a restaurant, a swimming pool or childcare. Some establishments have conference services and meeting rooms and encourage groups to hold conventions and meetings at their location.
Motel	Motel referred initially to a type of hotel in Columbia, MD of a single building of connected rooms

Go to **Cram101.com** for the Practice Tests for this Chapter.

whose doors faced a parking lot and, in some circumstances, a common area; or a series of small cabins with common parking.

Supply	The supply is the relationship between the quantity of goods supplied by the producers of a good and the current market price. It is graphically represented by the supply curve. It is commonly represented as directly proportional to price.
Wholesaling	Wholesaling is the sale of goods or merchandise to retailers, to industrial, commercial, institutional, or other professional business users, or to other wholesalers and related subordinated services.
Xerox	Xerox Corporation is a global document management company, which manufactures and sells a range of color and black-and-white printers, multifunction systems, photo copiers, digital production printing presses, and related consulting services and supplies.
Accessory equipment	Accessory equipment is any capital item that is less expensive and has a shorter life than an installation. This includes hand tools, computers, desk calculators, and forklifts. While some forms of accessory equipment are involved directly in the production process, most are indirectly involved.
Capital	Capital generally refers to financial wealth, especially that used to start or maintain a business. In classical economics, capital is one of four factors of production, the others being land and labor and entrepreneurship.
Capital equipment	In general terms, Capital equipment refers to equipment that is used by a business enterprise to manufacturer its products and provide a service. It is also used to sell, store and deliver merchandise. Capital equipment is not sold in the normal course of business, but will be used and worn out or consumed in the course of business.
Motorola	Motorola is an American multinational communications company based in Schaumburg, Illinois, a Chicago suburb. Motorola developed the first truly global communication network using a set of 66 satellites. The business ambitions behind this project and the need for raising venture capital to fund the project led to the creation of the Iridium company. Recently, it has ventured off to start a wireless phone service with Bradford Mobile Phones, and Kansas City Gold.
Nokia Corporation	Nokia Corporation is a Finnish multinational communications corporation, focused on the key growth areas of wired and wireless telecommunications. It is currently the world's largest manufacturer of mobile telephones, with a global device market share of approximately 39% in Q3. It comprises four business groups: Mobile Phones, Multimedia, Enterprise Solutions and Networks, plus various horizontal entities such as Customer and Market Operations, and Technology Platforms.
Raw material	A Raw material is something that is acted upon by human labor or industry to create some product that humans desire. Often the term is used to denote material that came from nature and is still in a unprocessed or minimally processed state.
Strategic planning	The process of determining the major goals of the organization and the policies and strategies for obtaining and using resources to achieve those goals is called strategic planning. Strategic Planning is the formal consideration of an organization's future course.
Maintenance, repair, and operations	Maintenance, Repair, and Operations is fixing any sort of mechanical or electrical device should it get out of order or broken (repair) as well as performing the routine actions which keep the device in working order (maintenance) or prevent trouble from arizing (preventive maintenance).
Materials	Materials are physical substances used as inputs to production or manufacturing. Materials range from man made synthetics such as many plastics to natural materials such as copper or wood.
Planning	Planning is both the organizational process of creating and maintaining a plan; and the psychological process of thinking about the activities required to create a desired future on some scale.

Service	In economics and marketing, a service is the non-material equivalent of a good. Service has been defined as an economic activity that does not result in ownership, and this is what differentiates it from providing physical goods.
Alcatel	Alcatel-Lucent is a French company that provides hardware, software, and services to telecommunications service providers and enterprises all over the globe.
Coca-Cola	Coca-Cola is the world's most recognizable brand, according to BusinessWeek. The first serving in 1886 cost US$0.05. The Coca-Cola is the world's largest consumer of natural vanilla extract. The exact formula of Coca-Cola is a famous trade secret. The original copy of the formula is held in SunTrust Bank's main vault in Atlanta.
Ericsson	Ericsson is a leading Swedish-based provider of telecommunication and data communication systems, and related services covering a range of technologies, including handset technology platforms. It has played an important global role in modernizing exising copper lines to offer broadband services and has actively grown a new line of business in the professional services area. By outsourcing certain activities to Ericsson, operators focus on their core business of attracting, serving and retaining customers.
Ford	Ford is an American company that manufactures and sells automobiles worldwide. Ford introduced methods for large-scale manufacturing of cars, and large-scale management of an industrial workforce, especially elaborately engineered manufacturing sequences typified by the moving assembly lines.
Nortel	Nortel is a multinational telecommunications equipment manufacturer headquartered in Toronto, Canada. This company was incorporated as the Northern Electric and Manufacturing Company Limited. Nortel is a long established industry leader in delivering end-to-end carrier grade telecommunications network infrastructure and solutions. The company has decades of experience in delivering robust, fault tolerant, software architectures and the know-how to scale to millions of users and manage thousands of network elements.
Airline	An airline provides air transport services for passengers or freight, generally with a recognized operating certificate or license. An Airline will lease or own their aircraft with which to supply these services and may form partnerships or alliances with other airline companies for mutual benefit.
CEMEX	Cemex SAB de CV is the world's largest building materials supplier and third largest cement producer. The company has operations extending around the world, including production facilities in 50 countries in North America, the Caribbean, South America, Europe, Asia, and Africa.
Delta Airlines	Delta Airlines is a major American airline headquartered in Atlanta, Georgia that operates an expansive domestic and international network. It is the sixth-largest airline in the world. It filed for Chapter 11 bankruptcy protection for the first time in its 76-year history. The company cited high labor costs and record-breaking jet fuel prices as factors in its filing. At the time of the filing, it had $20.5 billion in debt, $10 billion of which accumulated since January 2001.
Instrument	Instrument refers to an economic variable that is controlled by policy makers and can be used to influence other variables, called targets. Examples are monetary and fiscal policies used to achieve external and internal balance.
Texas Instruments	Texas Instruments is an American company based in Dallas, Texas, USA, renowned for developing and commercializing semiconductor and computer technology. Texas Instruments had two interesting problems with engineering and product development after the introduction of the semiconductor and the microprocessor.
United States Navy	The United States Navy is the branch of the United States armed forces responsible for conducting naval operations and is one of seven uniformed services. The U.S. Navy currently has over 335,000 personnel on active duty and 128,000 in the Navy Reserve. It operates 280 ships in active service

	and more than 3,700 aircraft.
Purchasing	Purchasing refers to a business or organization attempting to acquire goods or services to accomplish the goals of the enterprise. Though there are several organizations that attempt to set standards in the purchasing process, processes can vary greatly between organizations.
Demand	The demand represents the amount of a good that buyers are willing and able to purchase at various prices, assuming all other non-price factors remain the same. The demand curve is almost always represented as downwards-sloping, meaning that as price decreases, consumers will buy more of the good.
Derived demand	Derived demand is a term in economics, where demand for one good or service occurs as a result of demand for another. This may occur as the former is a part of production of the second. Derived demand applies to both consumers and producers. Producers have a derived demand for employees, the employees themselves are not demanded, rather the skills and productivity that they bring.
Volatility	Volatility refers to the extent to which a variable, such as a price or an exchange rate, moves up and down over time.
Price elasticity of demand	In economics and business studies, the price elasticity of demand is an elasticity that measures the nature and degree of the relationship between changes in quantity demanded of a good and changes in its price.
Elasticity	In economics, elasticity is the ratio of the incremental percentage change in one variable with respect to an incremental percentage change in another variable. Elasticity is usually expressed as a positive number (i.e., an absolute value) when the sign is already clear from context.
Inelastic	Inelastic refers to having an elasticity less than one. For a price elasticity of demand, this means that expenditure falls as price falls. For an income elasticity, it means that expenditure share falls with income.
Atkins Nutritionals	Atkins Nutritionals produces low-carbohydrate packaged foods.
Bruce Einhorn	Bruce Einhorn is a regional editor for BusinessWeek's Hong Kong bureau. He was the Asia technology correspondent for BusinessWeek. When he first became a part of the BusinessWeek staff, Einhorn joined as a Taiwan stringer in 1993.
Intel	Intel is the world's largest semiconductor company and the inventor of the x86 series of microprocessors, the processors found in many personal computers. After 2000, growth in demand for high-end microprocessors slowed and competitors garnered significant market share, initially in low-end and mid-range processors but ultimately across the product range, and it's dominant position was reduced. Intel has become one of the world's most recognizable computer brands following its long-running "Intel Inside" campaign.
Starbucks	Starbucks is a dominant multinational coffeehouse chain based in the United States. Starbucks does not franchise with individuals within North America but does enter into licensing arrangements with some companies. It entered the music industry with the acquisition of Hear Music, and the film industry with the creation of Starbucks Entertainment. This feature will slowly be offered in limited markets.
Value	Value of a product within the context of marketing means the relationship between the consumer's expectations of product quality to the actual amount paid for it. It can be defined by both qualitative and quantitative measures. On the qualitative side, value is the perceived gain composed of individual's emotional, mental and physical condition plus various social, economic, cultural and environmental factors. On the quantitative side, value is the actual gain measured in terms of financial numbers, percentages, and dollars.
Competitiveness	Competitiveness is a comparative concept of the ability and performance of a firm, sub-sector or

Go to **Cram101.com** for the Practice Tests for this Chapter.

country to sell and supply goods and/or services in a given market. The term may also be applied to markets, where it is used to refer to the extent to which the market structure may be regarded as perfectly competitive.

Competitive advantage	Competitive advantage is a position that a firm occupies in its competitive landscape. Michael Porter posits that a competitive advantage, sustainable or not, exists when a company makes economic rents, that is, their earnings exceed their costs. Most forms of competitive advantage cannot be sustained for any length of time because the promise of economic rents drives competitors to duplicate the competitive advantage held by any one firm.
Value chain	The Value chain is a concept from business management that was first described and popularized by Michael Porter in his 1985 best-seller, Competitive Advantage: Creating and Sustaining Superior Performance.

12

Go to **Cram101.com** for the Practice Tests for this Chapter.

Cessna	Cessna is a manufacturer of general aviation aircraft, primarily specializing in small, piston-powered aircraft and medium-sized business jets. They always had an active marketing department, notable during the 1950s and 1960s.
Textron	Textron today is a multi-industry company with a portfolio of familiar brands such as Bell Helicopter, E-Z-GO, Cessna Aircraft, and Greenlee, among others. With total revenues of $10 billion, and more than 37,000 employees in nearly 33 countries, Textron is headquartered in Providence, RI, USA, and currently ranked 190th on the Fortune 500 list of largest companies
Alcoa	Alcoa is the world's third largest producer of aluminum. Alcoa leads the world in alumina production and capacity. In addition to aluminum products, Alcoa also makes and markets consumer brands including Reynolds Wrap foil and plastic wrap, Baco household wraps, and Alcoa wheels. It is followed closely by a former subsidiary, Alcan, a Canadian-based company in Montreal, which was the third-leading producer behind Alcoa, but in terms of sales Alcan
Honeywell	Honeywell is a major American multinational conglomerate company that produces a variety of consumer products, engineering services, and aerospace systems for a wide variety of customers, from private consumers to major corporations. Honeywell originally entered the computer business via a joint venture with Raytheon called Datamatic Corp., but soon bought out Raytheon's share and the business became a Honeywell division.
Boeing	Boeing is the world's largest aircraft manufacturer by revenue. Headquartered in Chicago, Illinois, Boeing is the second-largest defense contractor in the world. In 2005, the company was the world's largest civil aircraft manufacturer in terms of value.
Office Depot	Office Depot is one of the world's leading suppliers of office products and services. The Company sells its products through multiple distribution channels, including over 1,000 office supply stores, direct mail, Internet websites, business-to-business e-commerce, and sales forces.
Buyer	A buyer is any person who contracts to acquire an asset in return for some form of consideration.
Market	A market is, as defined in economics, a social arrangement that allows buyers and sellers to discover information and carry out a voluntary exchange of goods or services.
Radio commercial	A radio commercial is a form of advertizing in which goods, services, organizations, ideas, etc. are promoted via the medium of radio.
Spot market	The spot market or is a commodities or securities market in which goods are sold for cash and delivered immediately.
Supply	The supply is the relationship between the quantity of goods supplied by the producers of a good and the current market price. It is graphically represented by the supply curve. It is commonly represented as directly proportional to price.
Supply chain	A supply chain, logistics network, or supply network is the system of organizations, people, activities, information and resources involved in moving a product or service from suppli-er to customer. Supply chain activities transform raw materials and components into a finished product that is delivered to the end customer.
Supply chain management	Supply chain management is the process of planning, implementing, and controlling the operations of the supply chain with the purpose to satisfy customer requirements as efficiently as possible. Supply chain management spans all movement and storage of raw materials, work-in-process inventory, and finished goods from point-of-origin to point-of-consumption.
Efficiency	Efficiency is a general term for the value assigned to a situation by some measure designed to reduce the amount of waste or "friction" or other undesirable economic features present.

Gain	In finance, gain is a profit or an increase in value of an investment such as a stock or bond. Gain is calculated by fair market value or the proceeds from the sale of the investment minus the sum of the purchase price and all costs associated with it.
Management	Management comprises directing and controlling a group of one or more people or entities for the purpose of coordinating and harmonizing that group towards accomplishing a goal. Management often encompasses the deployment and manipulation of human resources, financial resources, technological resources, and natural resources.
Hewlett-Packard	Hewlett-Packard is currently the world's largest information technology corporation and is known worldwide for its printers, personal computers and high end servers. The company, which once catered primarily to engineering and medical markets—a line of business it spun off as Agilent Technologies in 1999 now markets to households and small business. It is acknowledged by Wired magazine as the producer of the world's first personal computer, in 1968, the Hewlett-Packard 9100A.
Effectiveness	Effectiveness means the capability of producing an effect.
Relationship management	Relationship management is a broad term that covers concepts used by companies to manage their relationships with customers, including the capture, storage and analysis of customer, vendor, partner, and internal process information.
Motivation	Motivation is the reason or reasons for engaging in a particular behavior, especially human behavior as studied in psychology and neuropsychology. The reasons may include basic needs such as food or a desired object, goal, state of being, or ideal. The motivation for a behavior may also be attributed to less-apparent reasons such as altruism or morality. According to Geen, motivation refers to the initiation, direction, intensity and persistence of human behavior.
Exchange	The trade of things of value between buyer and seller so that each is better off after the trade is called the exchange.
Customer	Customer is someone who makes use of or receives the products or services of an individual or organization.
Customer relationship management	Customer relationship management is a term applied to processes implemented by a company to handle their contact with their customers. Customer relationship management software is used to support these processes, storing information on customers and prospective customers.
Ariba	Ariba is software and information technology services company founded on the idea of using the Internet to enable companies to facilitate and improve the procurement process.
General Mills	General Mills is a corporation, mainly concerned with food products, which is headquartered in Golden Valley, Minnesota, a suburb of Minneapolis. The company markets such brands as Betty Crocker, Progresso, Yoplait, Old El Paso, and Pillsbury, as well as numerous well-known breakfast cereals. General Mills often uses product placement on Millsberry.
IBM	IBM is a multinational computer technology and consulting corporation. It manufactures and sells computer hardware, software, infrastructure services, hosting services and consulting services in areas ranging from mainframe computers to nanotechnology.
Spot price	The spot price of a commodity, a security or a currency is the price that is quoted for immediate settlement. Spot settlement is normally one or two business days from trade date.
Verizon	Verizon a Dow 30 company, is a broadband and telecommunications provider. The acquisition of GTE by Bell Atlantic, on June 30, 2000, which formed Verizon, was among the largest mergers in United States business history. Verizon, with MCI, is currently the second largest telecommunications company in the United States.
Interest	In finance and economics, interest is the price paid by a borrower for the use of a lender's

money. In other words, interest is the amount of paid to "rent" money for a period of time.

Television advertisement

A television advertisement is a form of advertising in which goods, services, organizations, ideas, etc. are promoted via the medium of television.

Corporation

A corporation is a legal entity which has a separate legal personality from its members. The defining legal rights and obligations of the corporation are: the ability to sue and be sued; the ability to hold assets in its own name; the ability to hire agents; the ability to sign contracts; and the ability to make by-laws, which govern its internal affairs.

Credit

Credit refers to a recording as positive in the balance of payments, any transaction that gives rise to a payment into the country, such as an export, the sale of an asset, or borrowing from abroad.

Strategic partnership

A strategic partnership is a formal alliance between two commercial enterprises, usually formalized by one or more business contracts but falls short of forming a legal partnership or, agency, or corporate affiliate relationship.

Xerox

Xerox Corporation is a global document management company, which manufactures and sells a range of color and black-and-white printers, multifunction systems, photo copiers, digital production printing presses, and related consulting services and supplies.

Partnership

A partnership is a type of business entity in which partners share with each other the profits or losses of the business undertaking in which all have invested.

Instrument

Instrument refers to an economic variable that is controlled by policy makers and can be used to influence other variables, called targets. Examples are monetary and fiscal policies used to achieve external and internal balance.

Intel

Intel is the world's largest semiconductor company and the inventor of the x86 series of microprocessors, the processors found in many personal computers. After 2000, growth in demand for high-end microprocessors slowed and competitors garnered significant market share, initially in low-end and mid-range processors but ultimately across the product range, and it's dominant position was reduced. Intel has become one of the world's most recognizable computer brands following its long-running "Intel Inside" campaign.

Motorola

Motorola is an American multinational communications company based in Schaumburg, Illinois, a Chicago suburb. Motorola developed the first truly global communication network using a set of 66 satellites. The business ambitions behind this project and the need for raising venture capital to fund the project led to the creation of the Iridium company. Recently, it has ventured off to start a wireless phone service with Bradford Mobile Phones, and Kansas City Gold.

Palm

Palm is a personal digital assistant manufacturer headquartered in Sunnyvale, California that is responsible for popular products such as the Zire, Tungsten PDAs, Treo smartphones and the LifeDrive.

Texas Instruments

Texas Instruments is an American company based in Dallas, Texas, USA, renowned for developing and commercializing semiconductor and computer technology. Texas Instruments had two interesting problems with engineering and product development after the introduction of the semiconductor and the microprocessor.

Preference

Preference (or "taste") is a concept, used in the social sciences, particularly economics. It assumes a real or imagined "choice" between alternatives and the possibility of rank ordering of these alternatives, based on happiness, satisfaction, gratification, enjoyment, utility they provide.

Unisys

Unisys Corporation, based in Blue Bell, Pennsylvania, United States, and incorporated in Delaware, is a global provider of information technology services and solutions.

Awareness	In biological psychology, awareness comprises a human's or an animal's perception and cognitive reaction to a condition or event. It may also refer to public or common knowledge or understanding about a social, scientific, or political issue, and hence many movements try to foster "awareness" of a given subject.
Robert Dwyer	Robert Dwyer is the Joseph S. Stern Professor of Marketing at the University of Cincinnati. His main areas of interest focus on interfirm governance and the development of relationships between buyers and sellers. He currently serves on the editorial review board for the Journal of Business and Industrial Marketing, Journal of Marketing Channels, and the Journal of B2B Marketing.
Bargaining	Bargaining is a type of negotiation in which the buyer and seller of a good or service dispute the price which will be paid and the exact nature of the transaction that will take place, and eventually come to an agreement. Bargaining is an alternative pricing strategy to fixed prices.
Reciprocation	Reciprocation is the action in which a body's displacement returns to its starting location in a given time repeatedly.
Justice	Justice concerns the proper ordering of things and persons within a society. As a concept it has been subject to philosophical, legal, and theological reflection and debate throughout history.
Norm	In sociology, a norm is a rule that is socially enforced. Social sanctioning is what distinguishes them from other cultural products or social constructions such as meaning and values. They and normlessness are thought to affect a wide variety of human behavior.
Power	Much of the recent sociological debate on power revolves around the issue of the enabling nature of power.
Outsourcing	Outsourcing refers to the delegation of non-core operations from internal production to an external entity specializing in the management of that operation. Outsourcing is utilizing experts from outside the entity to perform specific tasks that the entity once performed itself.
Trust	An arrangement in which shareholders of independent firms agree to give up their stock in exchange for trust certificates that entitle them to a share of the trust's common profits.
Chrysler	Chrysler is an American automobile manufacturer. Chrysler is now the largest private automaker in North America. A joint venture with Mitsubishi called Diamond Star Motors strengthened the company's hand in the small car market. Chrysler acquired AMC primarily for its Jeep brand, although the failing Eagle Premier would be the basis for the Chrysler LH platform sedans. This bolstered the firm, although Chrysler was still the weakest of the Big Three.
Ford	Ford is an American company that manufactures and sells automobiles worldwide. Ford introduced methods for large-scale manufacturing of cars, and large-scale management of an industrial workforce, especially elaborately engineered manufacturing sequences typified by the moving assembly lines.
Dissolution	Dissolution is the process of admitting or removing a partner in a partnership.
Commitment	Personal commitment is the act or quality of voluntarily taking on or fulfilling obligations. What makes personal commitment "personal" is the voluntary aspect. In particular, it is not necessary that a personal commitment relate to personal interests.
Samsung	On November 30, 2005 Samsung pleaded guilty to a charge it participated in a worldwide DRAM price fixing conspiracy during 1999-2002 that damaged competition and raized PC prices.
Verification	Verification refers to the final stage of the creative process where the validity or

truthfulness of the insight is determined. The feedback portion of communication in which the receiver sends a message to the source indicating receipt of the message and the degree to which he or she understood the message.

Cross-cultural	The process of educating employees who are given an assignment in a foreign country is cross-cultural preparation.
Integration	Economic integration refers to reducing barriers among countries to transactions and to movements of goods, capital, and labor, including harmonization of laws, regulations, and standards. Integrated markets theoretically function as a unified market.
Vertical integration	Vertical integration describes a style of ownership and control. The degree to which a firm owns its upstream suppliers and its downstream buyers determines how vertically integrated it is. Vertical integration is one method of avoiding the hold-up problem.
Contract	A contract is a "promise" or an "agreement" that is enforced or recognized by the law. In the civil law, a contract is considered to be part of the general law of obligations.
Pledge	In law a pledge (also pawn) is a bailment of personal property as a security for some debt or engagement.
Rochester Products Division	Rochester Products Division was a division of General Motors that manufactured carburetors, and related components including emissions control devices and cruise control systems in Rochester, New York. It began as North East Electric Company in the 1800's. They are famous for their highly regarded Quadrajet carburetor, which was originally designed in the 1960s and due to extraordinary engineering, met emissons standards into the 1980s.
Network	Economic network or refereed network of independent individuals has the primary purpose of making a strong community in order to gain strength and perform as a significant player in relation to current market situation. Activities of economic network consist also of recruiting new members to join, reviewing, surveying, or providing a fresh perspective on existing community growth and strength.
Social	Social refers to human society or its organization.
Social relation	Social relation can refer to a multitude of social interactions, regulated by social norms, between two or more people, with each having a social position and performing a social role.
Cisco	Cisco designs and sells networking and communications technology and services under five brands, namely Cisco, Linksys, WebEx, IronPort, and Scientific Atlanta. Initially, Cisco manufactured only enterprise multi-protocol routers but gradually diversified its product offering to move into the home user market with the purchase of Linksys while also expanding its offering for corporate customers.
Dow Corning	Dow Corning is a multinational corporation specialized in silicon and silicone-based technology, offering more than 7,000 products and services. A large, majority-owned subsidiary of Dow Corning Corporation is the Hemlock Semiconductor Corporation. Class-action lawsuits claimed that it's silicone breast implants caused systemic health problems. The claims first centered around breast cancer, and then migrated to a range of autoimmune diseases, including lupus, rheumatoid arthritis and various neurological problems. This led to numerous lawsuits. As a result, Dow Corning was in bankruptcy protection for nine years,
Kroger	Kroger is an American retail supermarket chain and parent company, founded by Bernard Henry Kroger. It reported over US$60 billion in sales during its most recent fiscal year and is the top grocery retailer in the country and third-place general retailer in the country. As well as stocking a variety of national brand products, it also employs one of the largest networks of private label manufacturing in the country. A three-tiered marketing strategy divides the brand names for shoppers' simplicity and understanding.

Wal-Mart	Wal-Mart is an American public corporation, currently the world's 2nd largest corporation according to the 2007 Fortune 500. It was founded by Sam Walton in 1962.
George Washington Carver	George Washington Carver worked in agricultural extension at the Tuskegee Institute, in Tuskegee, Alabama, teaching former slaves farming techniques for self-sufficiency. His exact birth day are unknown, yet it is known that it was some time before slavery was abolished in Missouri in January, 1865. To commemorate his life and inventions, George Washington Carver Recognition Day is celebrated every January 5, on the day Carver died.
Honda	Honda is a Japanese multinational corporation, engine manufacturer and engineering corporation. Honda is the largest engine-maker in the world, producing more than 14 million internal combustion engines built each year. It was the first Japanese automaker to introduce a separate luxury line of vehicles. Many of it's most remarkable advertising campaigns have been released for the UK market, and have not been broadcast in North America except on the internet.
Marketing	Marketing is the process or act of bringing together buyers and sellers. Two major factors of marketing are the recruitment of new customers and the retention and expansion of relationships with existing customers. Marketing methods are informed by many of the social sciences, particularly psychology, sociology, and economics.
John Carey	John Carey was a U.S. Representative from Ohio.
ChemNutra	ChemNutra is a Summerlin, Nevada based importer of ingredients for food, animal feed and pharmaceuticals. Self-described as "The China-Source Experts" they import their products from China and provide them to North American manufacturers. The Chief Executive Officer is Stephen S. Miller and the president is Sally Miller.
Industry	Industry, is the segment of economy concerned with production of goods. Industry began in its present form during the 1800s, aided by technological advances, and it has continued to develop to this day.
Industrial Product	An industrial product is a good that is destined to be sold primarily for use in producing other goods or rendering services as contrasted with goods to be sold mainly to the ultimate consumer.
Just-in-Time	Just-In-Time is an inventory strategy implemented to improve the return on investment of a business by reducing in-process inventory and its associated costs. The process is driven by a series of signals, or Kanban, that tell production processes to make the next part.
Market Failure	Market failure is a term used by economists to describe the condition where the allocation of goods and services by a market is not efficient. Economists, especially microeconomists, use many different models and theorems to analyze the causes of market failure, and possible means to correct such a failure when it occurs. Such analysis plays an important role in many types of public policy decisions and studies.
Technology	Technology is a broad concept that deals with a species' usage and knowledge of tools and crafts, and how it affects a species' ability to control and adapt to its environment. In human society, it is a consequence of science and engineering, although several technological advances predate the two concepts.
Xuzhou Anying Biologic Technology Development	The Xuzhou Anying Biologic Technology Development Co. is a technological enterprise focused on research, production, distribution, which exports biologic feed, feed additive, edible flour, and agricultural and sideline products. Specifically, the company specializes in the export of wheat gluten, wheat flour, cornstarch, sweet potato starch, and other agricultural items.
Ravi Singh Achrol	Ravi Singh Achrol is the Professor of Strategic Marketing at the University of West Virginia. He is an accomplished author who has written extensively on the changing methods of marketing

Go to **Cram101.com** for the Practice Tests for this Chapter.

warfare from the 80's until the present. He has also written about dealing with suppliers as marketing conditions constantly shift and change.

Erin Anderson	Erin Anderson was the John H. Loudon Chaired Professor of International Management and Professor of Marketing at INSEAD, France, which she became a part of in 1994. Her research was mostly focused on issues regarding the motivation, structuring, and control of the sales force and channels of distribution.
Jan B. Heide	Jan B. Heide is the Irwin Maier Chair of Marketing at the UW-Madison School of Business. His areas of expertise include distribution channels, inter-organizational relationships, strategic decision-making, and vertical market restrictions. He received his Ph.D. from UW-Madison.
Thomas W. Speh	Dr. Thomas W. Speh is the James Evans Rees Distinguished Professor of Distribution and Associate Dean of the Richard T. Farmer School of Business Administration at Miami University in Ohio. He also teaches courses in Logistics Management and Supply Chain Management.
Shelby D. Hunt	Shelby D. Hunt is the Jerry S. Rawls and P. W. Horn Professor of Marketing. He was previously an editor for the Journal of Marketing from 1984-1987, and a chairman of the Marketing Department at the University of Wisconsin-Madison from 1974-1980.

Ericsson	Ericsson is a leading Swedish-based provider of telecommunication and data communication systems, and related services covering a range of technologies, including handset technology platforms. It has played an important global role in modernizing exising copper lines to
Purchasing	Purchasing refers to a business or organization attempting to acquire goods or services to accomplish the goals of the enterprise. Though there are several organizations that attempt to set standards in the purchasing process, processes can vary greatly between organizations.
Just-in-time	Just-In-Time is an inventory strategy implemented to improve the return on investment of a business by reducing in-process inventory and its associated costs. The process is driven by a series of signals, or Kanban, that tell production processes to make the next part.
PPG Industries	PPG Industries is an American manufacturer of glass and chemical products, including automotive safety glass. It is also the world's third largest producer of chlorine and caustic soda, vinyl chloride, and chlorinated solvents. It recently made an offer to Bain Capital to buy the SigmaKalon Group of companies, which produce paints and speciality coating.
Supply	The supply is the relationship between the quantity of goods supplied by the producers of a good and the current market price. It is graphically represented by the supply curve. It is commonly represented as directly proportional to price.
Concept	As the term is used in mainstream cognitive science and philosophy of mind, a concept is an abstract idea or a mental symbol, typically associated with a corresponding representation in and language or symbology.
Contribution	In business organization law, the cash or property contributed to a business by its owners is referred to as contribution.
Boeing	Boeing is the world's largest aircraft manufacturer by revenue. Headquartered in Chicago, Illinois, Boeing is the second-largest defense contractor in the world. In 2005, the company was the world's largest civil aircraft manufacturer in terms of value.
Church	A church is an association of people with a common belief system, especially one that is based on the teachings of Jesus of Nazareth.
Deere and Company	Deere and Company is an American corporation based in Moline, Illinois, and the leading manufacturer of agricultural machinery in the world. It currently stands at 98th rank in Fortune 500 ranking. Deere and Company agricultural products, usually sold under the John Deere name, include tractors, combine harvesters, balers, planters/seeders, ATVs and forestry equipment. The company is also a leading supplier of construction equipment, as well as equipment used in lawn, grounds and turf care, such as ride-on lawn mowers, string trimmers, chainsaws, snowthrowers and for a short period, snowmobiles.
Electronic data interchange	Electronic Data Interchange is a set of standards for structuring information that is to be electronically exchanged between and within businesses, organizations, government entities and other groups. The standards describe structures that emulate documents, for example purchase orders to automate purchasing.
Ford	Ford is an American company that manufactures and sells automobiles worldwide. Ford introduced methods for large-scale manufacturing of cars, and large-scale management of an industrial workforce, especially elaborately engineered manufacturing sequences typified by the moving assembly lines.
Manufacturing	Manufacturing is the use of tools and labor to make things for use or sale. The term may refer to a vast range of human activity, from handicraft to high tech, but is most commonly applied to industrial production, in which raw materials are transformed into finished goods on a large scale.

Quality	In everyday language, business, engineering and manufacturing, quality consists of the characteristics of a product or service that bear on its ability to satisfy stated or implied needs; a product or service free of deficiencies.
Outsourcing	Outsourcing refers to the delegation of non-core operations from internal production to an external entity specializing in the management of that operation. Outsourcing is utilizing experts from outside the entity to perform specific tasks that the entity once performed itself.
Total cost	Total cost describes the total economic cost of production and is made up of variable costs, which according to quantity produced such as raw materials, plus fixed costs, which are independant of quanity produced such as expenses for assets like buildings.
Total cost of ownership	Total cost of ownership is a financial estimate designed to help consumers and enterprise managers assess direct and indirect costs commonly related to software or hardware.
Cost	In economics, business, and accounting, a cost is the value of money that has been used up to produce something.
Ownership	Ownership is the state or fact of exclusive rights and control over property, which may be an object, land/real estate, intellectual property or some other kind of property. It is embodied in an ownership right also referred to as title.
Complexity	The complexity of a particular system is the degree of difficulty in predicting the properties of the system if the properties of the system's parts are given.
Forward buying	Forward buying refers to a response to discounts offered by manufacturers in which retailers purchase more merchandise than they plan to sell during the promotion. The remaining stock is sold at a regular price later, or diverted to another store.
Value	Value of a product within the context of marketing means the relationship between the consumer's expectations of product quality to the actual amount paid for it. It can be defined by both qualitative and quantitative measures. On the qualitative side, value is the perceived gain composed of individual's emotional, mental and physical condition plus various social, economic, cultural and environmental factors. On the quantitative side, value is the actual gain measured in terms of financial numbers, percentages, and dollars.
Value analysis	Value analysis refers to a systematic appraisal of the design, quality, and performance of a product to reduce purchasing costs.
Analysis	Analysis means literally to break a complex problem down into smaller, more manageable "independent" parts for the purposes of examination — with the hope that solving these smaller parts will lead to a solution of the more complex problem as well.
Management	Management comprises directing and controlling a group of one or more people or entities for the purpose of coordinating and harmonizing that group towards accomplishing a goal. Management often encompasses the deployment and manipulation of human resources, financial resources, technological resources, and natural resources.
Emerson Electric	Emerson Electric manufactured electric motors and fans using an electric motor patented by the Meston brothers. It quickly expanded its product line to include electric sewing machines, electric dental drills, and power tools. It also an appliance market competitor with General Electric, the owner of NBC.
Partnership	A partnership is a type of business entity in which partners share with each other the profits or losses of the business undertaking in which all have invested.
R. R. Donnelley	R. R. Donnelley provides print and related services. In the late 1980s, the division was spun off as its own company, Geosystems, which in turn became MapQuest and is now a subsidiary of Time Warner.

Supply chain	A supply chain, logistics network, or supply network is the system of organizations, people, activities, information and resources involved in moving a product or service from suppli-er to customer. Supply chain activities transform raw materials and components into a finished product that is delivered to the end customer.
System	System is a set of interacting or interdependent entities, real or abstract, forming an integrated whole.
Department of Defense	The Department of Defense is the federal department charged with coordinating and supervising all agencies and functions of the government relating directly to national security and the military.
Single sourcing	Single sourcing is the origination of any design, set of concepts, or any article real or insubstantial from a single, well defined source, either a person or an organization.
Sourcing	In business, the term word sourcing refers to a number of procurement practices, aimed at finding, evaluating and engaging suppliers of goods and services.
Supplier evaluation	Supplier evaluation is a term used in business and refers to the process of evaluating and approving potential suppliers by factual and measurable assesment. The purpose of supplier evaluation is to ensure a portfolio of best in class suppliers is available for use.
Evaluation	Evaluation is the systematic determination of merit, worth, and significance of something or someone. Evaluation often is used to characterize and appraise subjects of interest in a wide range of human enterprises, including the Arts, business, computer science, criminal justice, engineering, foundations and non-profit organizations, government, health care, and other human services.
Buyclass framework	The term Buyclass framework refers to a classification of different procurement situations in an enterprise involving management economics.
Straight rebuy	A straight rebuy is the purchase of standard parts; maintenance, repair, and operating items; or any recurring need that is handled on a routine basis. It can be the purchase of the same goods in the same quantity on the same terms form the same supplier.
Modified rebuy	A buying situation in which the users, influencers, or deciders in the buying center want to change the product specifications, price, delivery schedule, or supplier is a modified rebuy.
Marketing	Marketing is the process or act of bringing together buyers and sellers. Two major factors of marketing are the recruitment of new customers and the retention and expansion of relationships with existing customers. Marketing methods are informed by many of the social sciences, particularly psychology, sociology, and economics.
Practice	Most commonly, practice is a learning method, the act of rehearsing a behavior over and over, or engaging in an activity again and again, for the purpose of improving or mastering it, as in the phrase "practice makes perfect". Sports teams practice to prepare for actual games. Playing a musical instrument well takes a lot of practice.
Xerox	Xerox Corporation is a global document management company, which manufactures and sells a range of color and black-and-white printers, multifunction systems, photo copiers, digital production printing presses, and related consulting services and supplies.
Corporation	A corporation is a legal entity which has a separate legal personality from its members. The defining legal rights and obligations of the corporation are: the ability to sue and be sued; the ability to hold assets in its own name; the ability to hire agents; the ability to sign contracts; and the ability to make by-laws, which govern its internal affairs.
Dell	Dell develops, manufactures, sells and supports personal computers, servers, data storage devices, network switches, personal digital assistants, software, televisions, computer peripherals and other technology-related products.

Go to **Cram101.com** for the Practice Tests for this Chapter.

Hewlett-Packard	Hewlett-Packard is currently the world's largest information technology corporation and is known worldwide for its printers, personal computers and high end servers. The company, which once catered primarily to engineering and medical markets—a line of business it spun off as Agilent Technologies in 1999 now markets to households and small business. It is acknowledged by Wired magazine as the producer of the world's first personal computer, in 1968, the Hewlett-Packard 9100A.
Conjoint analysis	Conjoint analysis is a statistical technique used in market research to determine how people value different features that make up an individual product or service. The objective of conjoint analysis is to determine what combination of a limited number of attributes is most influential on respondent choice or decision making.
Incentive	An incentive is any factor (financial or non-financial) that provides a motive for a particular course of action, or counts as a reason for preferring one choice to the alternatives.
Honeywell	Honeywell is a major American multinational conglomerate company that produces a variety of consumer products, engineering services, and aerospace systems for a wide variety of customers, from private consumers to major corporations. Honeywell originally entered the computer business via a joint venture with Raytheon called Datamatic Corp., but soon bought out Raytheon's share and the business became a Honeywell division.
Motorola	Motorola is an American multinational communications company based in Schaumburg, Illinois, a Chicago suburb. Motorola developed the first truly global communication network using a set of 66 satellites. The business ambitions behind this project and the need for raising venture capital to fund the project led to the creation of the Iridium company. Recently, it has ventured off to start a wireless phone service with Bradford Mobile Phones, and Kansas City Gold.
Northrop	The Northrop was a leading aircraft manufacturer of the United States. The company merged with Grumman to form Northrop Grumman in 1994.
Bethlehem Steel	During its life, Bethlehem Steel was one of the largest shipbuilding companies in the world and was one of the most powerful symbols of American manufacturing leadership. It was the second largest steel producer in the United States, but following its 2001 bankruptcy, the company was dissolved and the remaining assets sold to International Steel Group in 2003.
Demand	The demand represents the amount of a good that buyers are willing and able to purchase at various prices, assuming all other non-price factors remain the same. The demand curve is almost always represented as downwards-sloping, meaning that as price decreases, consumers will buy more of the good.
Supply chain management	Supply chain management is the process of planning, implementing, and controlling the operations of the supply chain with the purpose to satisfy customer requirements as efficiently as possible. Supply chain management spans all movement and storage of raw materials, work-in-process inventory, and finished goods from point-of-origin to point-of-consumption.
Planning	Planning is both the organizational process of creating and maintaining a plan; and the psychological process of thinking about the activities required to create a desired future on some scale.
Trend	Trend refers to the long-term movement of an economic variable, such as its average rate of increase or decrease over enough years to encompass several business cycles.
Globalization	Globalization refers to increasing global connectivity, integration and interdependence in the economic, social, technological, cultural, political, and ecological spheres.
Applied	Applied Materials, Inc. is the global leader in nanomanufacturing technology solutions with a

Materials	broad portfolio of innovative equipment, service and software products for the fabrication of semiconductor chips, flat panel solar displays, solar photovoltaic cells, flexible electronics and energy efficient glass.
Cisco	Cisco designs and sells networking and communications technology and services under five brands, namely Cisco, Linksys, WebEx, IronPort, and Scientific Atlanta. Initially, Cisco manufactured only enterprise multi-protocol routers but gradually diversified its product offering to move into the home user market with the purchase of Linksys while also expanding its offering for corporate customers.
Early supplier involvement	Early supplier involvement is a practice which focuses on the involvement of one or more selected suppliers with the buyer's product design team early in the product development process. The overall goal is to use the supplier's expertise and experience in the development of a product specification that is designed for effective and efficient product allocation.
Intel	Intel is the world's largest semiconductor company and the inventor of the x86 series of microprocessors, the processors found in many personal computers. After 2000, growth in demand for high-end microprocessors slowed and competitors garnered significant market share, initially in low-end and mid-range processors but ultimately across the product range, and it's dominant position was reduced. Intel has become one of the world's most recognizable computer brands following its long-running "Intel Inside" campaign.
Make-or-buy decision	A decision as to whether a product or service should be produced in-house or purchased from an outside supplier is a make-or-buy decision.
Materials	Materials are physical substances used as inputs to production or manufacturing. Materials range from man made synthetics such as many plastics to natural materials such as copper or wood.
Decision	A decision is a final product of a specific mental/cognitive process by an individual or group, which is called decision making, or in more detail, Inactive decision making, Reactive decision making, and Proactive decision making. Therefore it is a subjective concept. It is a mental object and can be an opinion, a rule or a task for execution/application.
Asia	Asia is the world's largest and most populous continent. It covers 8.6% of the Earth's total surface area and, with almost 4 billion people, it contains more than 60% of the world's current human population.
Kingfisher	Kingfisher refers to small bright colored birds of the three families Alcedinidae, Halcyonidae, and Cerylidae which lives near water.
Peak	Peak refers to the point in the business cycle when an economic expansion reaches its highest point before turning down. Contrasts with trough.
Supplier relationship management	Supplier relationship management is an information system that automates sourcing, purchasing and the management of daily supplier relations. It provides modules for vendor identification and selection as well as direct procurement.
Relationship management	Relationship management is a broad term that covers concepts used by companies to manage their relationships with customers, including the capture, storage and analysis of customer, vendor, partner, and internal process information.
Minority	Minority is a sociological group that does not constitute a politically dominant plurality of the total population of a given society.
Government	A government is "the organization that is the governing authority of a political unit," "the ruling power in a political society," and the apparatus through which a governing body functions and exercises authority.

Subcontractor	A subcontractor is an individual or in many cases a business that signs a contract to perform part or all of the obligations of another's contract. It is hired by a general contrator to perform a specific task as part of the overall project. Whilst the most common concept of a subcontractor is in building works and civil engineering, the range of opportunities for subcontractor is much wider and it is possible that the greatest number now operate in the information technology and information sectors of business.
Administration	In business, administration consists of the performance or management of business operations and thus the making or implementing of major decisions. Administration can be defined as the universal process of organising people and resources efficiently so as to direct activities toward common goals and objectives.
General Services Administration	The General Services Administration is an independent agency of the United States government, to help manage and support the basic functioning of federal agencies. It supplies products and communications for U.S. government offices, provides transportation and office space to federal employees, and develops government wide cost-minimizing policies, among other management tasks. Its stated mission is to "help federal agencies better serve the public by offering, at best value, superior workplaces, expert solutions, acquisition services and management policies."
Service	In economics and marketing, a service is the non-material equivalent of a good. Service has been defined as an economic activity that does not result in ownership, and this is what differentiates it from providing physical goods.
Cost-plus contract	A cost-plus contract is a contract framed in such a way that when the contractor finishes the agreed-upon work, they receive compensation equal to their expenses plus some bonus.
Fixed-price	Fixed-price is a phrase used to mean that no bargaining is allowed over the price of a good or, less commonly, a service.
Monitoring	Monitoring competence can be described as awareness of what you know.
National Aeronautics and Space Administration	The National Aeronautics and Space Administration is an agency of the United States government, responsible for the nation's public space program
Agreement	A gentlemen's agreement is an informal agreement between two or more parties. It may be written, oral, or simply understood as part of an unspoken agreement by convention or through mutually beneficial etiquette. The essence of a gentleman's agreement is that it relies upon the honor of the parties for its fulfilment, rather than being in any way enforceable. It is, therefore, distinct from a legal agreement or contract, which can be enforced if necessary.
Contract	A contract is a "promise" or an "agreement" that is enforced or recognized by the law. In the civil law, a contract is considered to be part of the general law of obligations.
American Public Works Association	The American Public Works Association is an international, educational, and professional association of public agencies, private sector companies and individuals that provide public works goods and services. APWA was founded in 1938 and remains the oldest and largest organization of its kind worldwide with more than 25,000 members. The APWA currently consists of 67 chapters throughout North America.
Ethics	Ethics is a major branch of philosophy, encompasses right conduct and good life.
Code of ethics	A formal statement of ethical principles and rules of conduct is a code of ethics. Some may have the force of law; these are often promulgated by the (quasi-)governmental agency responsible for licensing a profession. Violations of these codes may be subject to administrative (e.g., loss of license), civil or penal remedies.

Go to **Cram101.com** for the Practice Tests for this Chapter.

Robert G. Cooper	Robert G. Cooper is an expert in the field of new product and product innovation management. He has been called "the quintessential scholar" in the field of new products in the Journal of Product Innovation Management. Robert has published 90 articles and six books on the topic, with a number of the articles winning awards.
Gift	A gift is the transfer of something, without the need for compensation that is involved in trade. A gift is a voluntary act which does not require anything in return. Even though it involves possibly a social expectation of reciprocity, or a return in the form of prestige or power, a gift is meant to be free.
IBM	IBM is a multinational computer technology and consulting corporation. It manufactures and sells computer hardware, software, infrastructure services, hosting services and consulting services in areas ranging from mainframe computers to nanotechnology.
Non-disclosure agreement	A non-disclosure agreement is a legal contract between at least two parties which outlines confidentiality materials the parties wish to share with one another for certain purposes, but wish to restrict from generalized use.
Susan Ariel Aaronson	Susan Ariel Aaronson is the Associate Research Professor of International Affairs at The Elliott School of International Affairs. Her areas of expertise are in international trade, business and human rights, business in conflict zones, economic growth and human rights, and global corporate social responsibility.

Go to **Cram101.com** for the Practice Tests for this Chapter.

Buying center	A buying center, in marketing, procurement, and organizational studies, is a group of employees responsible for purchasing an item for the organization.
Webex	Webex is a Cisco Systems, Inc. company that provides on-demand collaboration, online meeting, web conferencing and video conferencing applications. Its products include "Meeting Center", "Training Center", "Event Center", "Support Center", "Sales Center" "MeetMeNow", "PCNow",
Behavior	Behavior refers to the actions or reactions of an object or organism, usually in relation to the environment. Behavior can be conscious or unconscious, overt or covert, and voluntary or involuntary. In animals, behavior is controlled by the endocrine system and the nervous system.
Buyer	A buyer is any person who contracts to acquire an asset in return for some form of consideration.
Consumer behavior	Consumer behavior is the study of how people buy, what they buy, when they buy and why they buy. It blends elements from psychology, sociology, sociopsychology, anthropology and economics. It attempts to understand the buyer decision making process, both individually and in groups. It studies characteristics of individual consumers such as demographics, psychographics, and behavioral variables in an attempt to understand people's wants. It
Buyer decision process	A buyer decision process is the decision making processes undertaken by consumers in regard to a potential market transaction before, during, and after the purchase of a product or service.
Organizational buying behavior	The decision-making process that organizations use to establish the need for products and services and identify, evaluate, and choose among alternative brands and suppliers is an organizational buying behavior.
Cargill	Cargill, Incorporated is a privately held, multinational corporation, and is based in the state of Minnesota in the United States. It was founded in 1865, and has grown into the world's second largest privately held corporation.
Corporation	A corporation is a legal entity which has a separate legal personality from its members. The defining legal rights and obligations of the corporation are: the ability to sue and be sued; the ability to hold assets in its own name; the ability to hire agents; the ability to sign contracts; and the ability to make by-laws, which govern its internal affairs.
Market	A market is, as defined in economics, a social arrangement that allows buyers and sellers to discover information and carry out a voluntary exchange of goods or services.
Role	A role is a set of connected behaviors, rights and obligations as conceptualized by actors in a social situation. It is mostly defined as an expected behavior in a given individual social status and social position.
Role theory	Role theory is a perspective in social psychology that considers most of everyday activity to be living up to the roles, or expectations, of others.
Autonomy	Autonomy is the right to self-government. It refers to the capacity of a rational individual to make an informed, uncoerced decision.
Controller	Controller refers to the financial executive primarily responsible for management accounting and financial accounting. Also called chief accounting officer.
Decision	A decision is a final product of a specific mental/cognitive process by an individual or group, which is called decision making, or in more detail, Inactive decision making, Reactive decision making, and Proactive decision making. Therefore it is a subjective concept. It is a mental object and can be an opinion, a rule or a task for execution/application.
Influencer	Influencer marketing is a form of marketing that has emerged from a variety of recent

Go to **Cram101.com** for the Practice Tests for this Chapter.

marketing	practices and studies, in which focus is placed on specific key individuals rather than the target market as a whole
Purchasing	Purchasing refers to a business or organization attempting to acquire goods or services to accomplish the goals of the enterprise. Though there are several organizations that attempt to set standards in the purchasing process, processes can vary greatly between organizations.
Purchasing manager	A Purchasing Manager is an employee within a company, business or other organization who is responsible at some level for buying or approving the acquisition of goods and services needed by the company.
Users	Users refer to people in the organization who actually use the product or service purchased by the buying center.
Value and Lifestyles	Value and lifestyles is a well-known psychographic segmentation. It was developed in the 1970s to explain changing U.S. values and lifestyles. It has since been reworked to enhance its ability to predict consumer behavior. Segmentation research based on *value and lifestyles* is a product of SRI Consulting Business Intelligence.
Formal system	In formal logic, a formal system consists of a language and a set of inference rules, used to derive one expression from one or more other expressions antecedently supposed or derived. A formal system may be formulated and studied for its intrinsic properties, or it may be intended as a description of external phenomena.
Tektronix	Tektronix is a North American company best known for its test and measurement equipment such as oscilloscopes, logic analyzers, and video and mobile test protocol equipment. As of November 2007, Tektronix is a subsidiary of Danaher Corporation.
Advocate	An advocate is one who speaks on behalf of another person, especially in a legal context. An advocate is also a marketing term for a loyal client that recommends a product or service to their peers.
Champion	A champion is one who has repeatedly come out first among contestants in challenges or other test, one who is outstandingly skilled in their field.
Das Narayandas	Das Narayandas is the James J. Hill Professor of Business Administration at Harvard Business School. He is the current co-chair of HBS's Program for Leadership Development. His credentials include a Bachelor of Technology degree in Engineering from the Indian Institute of Technology, a Ph.D. in Management from Purdue University, and a Post-Graduate Diploma in Management from his studies at the Indian Institute of Management.
Marketing	Marketing is the process or act of bringing together buyers and sellers. Two major factors of marketing are the recruitment of new customers and the retention and expansion of relationships with existing customers. Marketing methods are informed by many of the social sciences, particularly psychology, sociology, and economics.
Financial risk	In essence financial risk is any risk associated with the usage of any type of financing.
Performance	A performance generally comprises an event in which one group of people behave in a particular way for another group of people.
Social	Social refers to human society or its organization.
Steelcase	Steelcase is an international office furniture company. The company at the time specialized in mainly file cabinets and safes. Steelcase was found at fault in a patent infringement suit brought against them by Haworth, Inc., another furniture company. Steelcase was ordered to pay $211.5 million in damages and interest.
Deere and Company	Deere and Company is an American corporation based in Moline, Illinois, and the leading manufacturer of agricultural machinery in the world. It currently stands at 98th rank in

	Fortune 500 ranking. Deere and Company agricultural products, usually sold under the John Deere name, include tractors, combine harvesters, balers, planters/seeders, ATVs and forestry equipment. The company is also a leading supplier of construction equipment, as well as equipment used in lawn, grounds and turf care, such as ride-on lawn mowers, string trimmers, chainsaws, snowthrowers and for a short period, snowmobiles.
Loyalty	Marketers tend to define customer loyalty as making repeat purchases. Some argue that it should be defined attitudinally as a strongly positive feeling about the brand.
Strategic planning	The process of determining the major goals of the organization and the policies and strategies for obtaining and using resources to achieve those goals is called strategic planning. Strategic Planning is the formal consideration of an organization's future course.
Choice theory	Choice theory is a discipline of analyzing the mathematical nature of the choice behavior of economic agents in microeconomics.
Planning	Planning is both the organizational process of creating and maintaining a plan; and the psychological process of thinking about the activities required to create a desired future on some scale.
Intrinsic reward	An intrinsic reward is a form of motivation that occurs from within the self; it is the ignited passion of enhancing job performance or learning new skills.
Self-orientation	Self-orientation is a psychological orientation where an individual desires to possess direct personal rewards regardless of the effects on others working with that individual. A self-oriented individual is characterized by dominating, introspective, and social insensitive behaviors. For example, athletes who have led highly successful careers tend to be self-orientated, whereas good coaches tend to be lower in self-orientation.
Valence	'Valence', as used in psychology, especially in discussing emotions, means the intrinsic attractiveness positive valence or aversiveness negative valence of an event, object, or situation
Reward	A psychological reward is a process that reinforces behavior — something that, when offered, causes a behavior to increase in intensity. Reward is an operational concept for describing the positive value an individual ascribes to an object, behavioral act or an internal physical state.
Defensive marketing warfare strategies	Defensive marketing warfare strategies are a type of marketing warfare strategy designed to protect a company's market share, profitability, product positioning, or mind share.
Self-efficacy	Self-efficacy is an impression that one is capable of performing in a certain manner or attaining certain goals. It is a belief that one has the capabilities to execute the courses of actions required to manage prospective situations.
Strategy	A strategy is a long term plan of action designed to achieve a particular goal, most often "winning". Strategy is differentiated from tactics or immediate actions with resources at hand by its nature of being extensively premeditated, and often practically rehearsed.
L.L. Bean	L.L. Bean is a privately held mail-order and retail company based in Freeport, Maine, specializing in clothing and outdoor equipment. L.L.Bean has a history of high quality manufacturing processes and products as well as excellent customer service.
SRI International	SRI International is one of the world's largest contract research institutes. It was founded as Stanford Research Institute in 1946 by the trustees of Stanford University as a center of innovation to support economic development in the region.

Colgate	Colgate, an oral hygiene product line and one of the namesake brands of the Colgate-Palmolive Company, is a manufacturer of a wide range of toothpastes and toothbrushes.
Lee	Lee is a brand of denim jeans founded in Salina, Kansas, headquartered in Kansas City, Kansas, U.S.A., and owned by the VF Corporation. Lee didn't become an important factor in its industry until when it conceived the Union-All.
Kirk Wakefield	Kirk Wakefield is a Professor of Marketing at the Baylor Business School.

48

Go to **Cram101.com** for the Practice Tests for this Chapter.

Federal Express	Federal Express is a cargo airline, printing, and courier company offering overnight courier, ground, heavy freight, document copying and logistics services.
Market	A market is, as defined in economics, a social arrangement that allows buyers and sellers to discover information and carry out a voluntary exchange of goods or services.
Market opportunity	A market opportunity emerges if a product, based on either one technology or several, fulfills the need of a market better than the competition and better than substitution-technologies within the given environmental frame.
L.L. Bean	L.L. Bean is a privately held mail-order and retail company based in Freeport, Maine, specializing in clothing and outdoor equipment. L.L.Bean has a history of high quality manufacturing processes and products as well as excellent customer service.
System	System is a set of interacting or interdependent entities, real or abstract, forming an integrated whole.
Account	In accountancy, an account is a label used for recording and reporting a quantity of almost anything. Most often it is a record of an amount of money owned or owed by or to a particular person or entity, or allocated to a particular purpose.
Customer	Customer is someone who makes use of or receives the products or services of an individual or organization.
Retention	In marketing & sales terminology : Sales retention is the department or the action needed to retain the current customers, subscribers.
BOSE	Bose is a privately-held American company based in Framingham, Massachusetts that specializes in audio equipment[2][3] and reinvests 100 percent of its profits back into the company. The company features products in Olympic stadiums, Broadway theaters, the Sistine Chapel and the Space Shuttle.
Enterprise	Enterprise refers to another name for a business organization. Other similar terms are business firm, sometimes simply business, sometimes simply firm, as well as company, and entity.
Lee	Lee is a brand of denim jeans founded in Salina, Kansas, headquartered in Kansas City, Kansas, U.S.A., and owned by the VF Corporation. Lee didn't become an important factor in its industry until when it conceived the Union-All.
Maximization	Maximization is an economics theory, that refers to individuals or societies gaining the maximum amount out of the resources they have available to theme theory proposed by most economists is that maximization refers to the maximization of profit.
James C. Anderson	James C. Anderson is Principal of James C. Anderson LLC, an international management consulting firm whose main focus is the implementation of customer value management at client firms. James is also the William L. Ford Distinguished Professor of Marketing and Wholesale Distribution at the Kellogg School of Management, Northwestern University, and a visiting professor of research at the School of Business, Public Administration, and Technology,
Data warehouse	A data warehouse is the main repository of an organization's historical data, its corporate memory. It contains the raw material for management's decision support system. The critical factor leading to the use of a data warehouse is that a data analyst can perform complex queries and analysis, such as data mining, on the information without slowing down the operational systems.
IBM	IBM is a multinational computer technology and consulting corporation. It manufactures and sells computer hardware, software, infrastructure services, hosting services and consulting services in areas ranging from mainframe computers to nanotechnology.

Dialogue	A dialogue is a reciprocal conversation between two or more entities.
Warehouse	Warehouse refers to a location, often decentralized, that a firm uses to store, consolidate, age, or mix stock; house product-recall programs; or ease tax burdens.
Loyalty	Marketers tend to define customer loyalty as making repeat purchases. Some argue that it should be defined attitudinally as a strongly positive feeling about the brand.
Decile	In descriptive statistics, a decile is any of the 9 values that divide the sorted data into 10 equal parts, so that each part represents 1/10th of the sample or population.
Report	A report is a document characterized by information or other content reflective of inquiry or investigation, which is tailored to the context of a given situation and audience.
Customer satisfaction research	Customer satisfaction research is that area of marketing research which focuses on customers' perceptions with their shopping or purchase experience.
Data mining	Data mining has been defined as "the nontrivial extraction of implicit, previously unknown, and potentially useful information from data" and "the science of extracting useful information from large data sets or databases" .
Focus	FOCUS is a software product of Information Builders Inc. Originally developed for data handling and analysis on the IBM mainframe, as newer systems were developed and smaller computers became more powerful, the available platforms for FOCUS were extended all the way down to personal computers and in 1997, to the Web in the WebFOCUS product.
Research	Research is a human activity based on intellectual investigation and aimed at discovering, interpreting, and revising human knowledge on different aspects of the world. Research can use the scientific method, but need not do so.
Sampling	Sampling is that part of statistical practice concerned with the selection of individual observations intended to yield some knowledge about a population of concern, especially for the purposes of statistical inference.
Interview	An interview is a conversation between two or more people where questions are asked by the interviewer to obtain information from the interviewee. Interviews can be divided into two rough types, interviews of assessment and interviews for information.
Abbie Griffin	Abbie Griffin is the Royal L. Garff Endowed Chair in Marketing in the David Eccles School of Business at the University of Utah. She received her bachelor's degree from Harvard University, and her Ph.D. in management of technology and marketing from MIT.
John R. Hauser	John R. Hauser is the Kirin Professor of Marketing and Head of the Marketing Group at the MIT Sloan School of Management. He is one of the founders of the field of Marketing Science and was Editor-in-Chief of the academic journal Marketing Science from 1989-1995.
Internet	In business, the internet is viewed as an essential marketing tool for the advertisement of products and services, as well as a very valuable source of maintaining customer contact and communication.
On-line and off-line	The terms on-line and off-line have specific meanings with respect to computer technology and telecommunication. The concepts have however been extended from their computing and telecommunication meanings into the area of human interaction and conversation.
Sugging	Sugging is a market research industry term, meaning "selling under the guise of research". This behavior occurs when a product marketer falsely pretends to be a market researcher conducting a survey, when in reality they are simply trying to sell the product in question.
Telephone survey	A telephone survey is a research method that involves calling customers/participants on the telephone to gather opnions regarding specific products and services provided by a company or

	affiliate.
Alcoa	Alcoa is the world's third largest producer of aluminum. Alcoa leads the world in alumina production and capacity. In addition to aluminum products, Alcoa also makes and markets consumer brands including Reynolds Wrap foil and plastic wrap, Baco household wraps, and Alcoa wheels. It is followed closely by a former subsidiary, Alcan, a Canadian-based company in Montreal, which was the third-leading producer behind Alcoa, but in terms of sales Alcan is ahead of Alcoa.
Customer acquisition	Customer Acquisition is a term used to describe the methodologies and systems to manage customer prospects and inquiries, generally generated by a variety of marketing techniques. It can be considered the connectivity between advertising and customer relationship management.
Acquisition	An acquisition, is the buying of one company by another. An acquisition may be friendly or hostile. In the former case, the companies cooperate in negotiations; in the latter case, the acquisition target is unwilling to be bought or the target's board has no prior knowledge of the offer. Acquisition usually refers to a purchase of a smaller firm by a larger one.
Lifetime value	In marketing, lifetime value is the present value of the future cash flows attributed to the customer relationship. Use of lifetime value as a marketing metric tends to place greater emphasis on customer service and long-term customer satisfaction, rather than on maximizing short-term sales.
Value	Value of a product within the context of marketing means the relationship between the consumer's expectations of product quality to the actual amount paid for it. It can be defined by both qualitative and quantitative measures. On the qualitative side, value is the perceived gain composed of individual's emotional, mental and physical condition plus various social, economic, cultural and environmental factors. On the quantitative side, value is the actual gain measured in terms of financial numbers, percentages, and dollars.
Mitsubishi	Mitsubishi is a Japanese conglomerate consisting of a range of autonomous businesses. It form a loose entity, the Mitsubishi Keiretsu, which is often referenced in US and Japanese media and official reports; in general these companies all descend from the zaibatsu of the same name. Later diversification carried the organization into such sectors as paper, steel, glass, electrical equipment, aircraft, oil, and real estate. As Mitsubishi built a broadly based conglomerate, it played a central role in the modernization of Japanese industry.
Morale	Morale when discussing the morale of a group, is an intangible term used for the capacity of people to maintain belief in an institution or a goal, or even in oneself and others. The second term applies particularly to military personnel and to members of sports teams, but is also applicable in business and in any other organizational context, particularly in times of stress or controversy.
Corporation	A corporation is a legal entity which has a separate legal personality from its members. The defining legal rights and obligations of the corporation are: the ability to sue and be sued; the ability to hold assets in its own name; the ability to hire agents; the ability to sign contracts; and the ability to make by-laws, which govern its internal affairs.
Grant	Grant refers to an intergovernmental transfer of funds . Since the New Deal, state and local governments have become increasingly dependent upon federal grants for an almost infinite variety of programs.
Thomas Register	Thomas Register, is a multi-volume directory of industrial product information covering 650,000 distributors, manufacturers and service companies within 67,000-plus industrial categories.
University of	The University of Michigan Document Center is a centralized reference and referral facility

Michigan Document Center	for government information, whether on the local, state, federal, foreign, or international level. The documents and web pages featured at the facility are utilized as reference and instructional tools for government, political science, news, and statistical data.
Role	A role is a set of connected behaviors, rights and obligations as conceptualized by actors in a social situation. It is mostly defined as an expected behavior in a given individual social status and social position.
Industry	Industry, is the segment of economy concerned with production of goods. Industry began in its present form during the 1800s, aided by technological advances, and it has continued to develop to this day.
Simon Majaro	Simon Majaro is a management author and was visiting professor at Cranfield School of Management. He has written several books on innovative management ideas such as The Essence of Marketing, The Creative Gap: Managing Ideas for Profit and International Marketing: A Strategic Approach to World Markets.
Market segment	A Market segment is a subgroup of people or organizations sharing one or more characteristics that cause them to have similar product needs.
North American Industrial Classification System	The North American Industrial Classification System is used by business and government to classify and measure economic activity in Canada, Mexico and the United States.
Standard Industrial Classification	The Standard Industrial Classification is a United States government system for classifying industries by a four-digit code.
Benefits	Employee benefits are various non-wage compensations provided to employees in addition to their normal wages or salaries. Where an employee exchanges cash wages for some other form of benefit, this is generally referred to as a 'salary sacrifice' arrangement. In most countries, most kinds of employee benefits are taxable to at least some degree.
Buyer decision process	A buyer decision process is the decision making processes undertaken by consumers in regard to a potential market transaction before, during, and after the purchase of a product or service.
Trade	A mechanism that allows trade is called a market. The original form of trade was barter, the direct exchange of goods and services. Modern traders instead generally negotiate through a medium of exchange, such as money.
Trade show	A trade show is an exhibition organized so tha companies in a specific industry can showcase and demostrate their new products and services. It often involve a considerable marketing investment by participating companies. Costs include space rental, display design and construction, telecommunications and networking, travel, accommodations, promotional literature, and "give away" items.
Positioning	The art and science of fitting the product or service to one or more segments of the market in such a way as to set it meaningfully apart from competition is called positioning.
Media	In communication, media are the storage and transmission tools used to store and deliver information or data. It is often referred to as synonymous with mass media or news media, but may refer to a single medium used to communicate any data for any purpose.
Accessibility	In transportation, accessibility refers to the ease of reaching destinations.
American Express	American Express is a diversified global financial services company. American Express became one of the monopolies that President Theodore Roosevelt had the Interstate Commerce Commission investigate during his administration. American Express acquired the investment

Go to **Cram101.com** for the Practice Tests for this Chapter.

	banking and trading firm, Lehman Brothers Kuhn Loeb, and added it to the Shearson family, creating Shearson Lehman/American Express.
Market share	Market share is the percentage or proportion of the total available market or market segment that is being services by a company. It can be expressed as a company's sales revenue divided by the total sales revenue available in that market. It can also be expressed as a company's unit sales volume divided by the total volume of units sold in that market.
Printing	Printing is a process for reproducing text and image, typically with ink on paper using a printing press. It is often carried out as a large-scale industrial process, and is an essential part of publishing and transaction printing.
Marketing research	Marketing Research is a form of business research and is generally divided into two categories: consumer market research and business-to-business market research, which was previously known as Industrial Marketing Research.
Robert C. Blattberg	Robert C. Blattberg is the Polk Brothers Distinguished Professor of Retailing at the Kellogg Graduate School of Management, Northwestern University. He also serves as the Chief Analytical Officer of Information Resources. Professor Blattberg's primary areas of research are database marketing, sales promotions, pricing and retailing.
Robert Dwyer	Robert Dwyer is the Joseph S. Stern Professor of Marketing at the University of Cincinnati. His main areas of interest focus on interfirm governance and the development of relationships between buyers and sellers. He currently serves on the editorial review board for the Journal of Business and Industrial Marketing, Journal of Marketing Channels, and the Journal of B2B Marketing.
Jiawei Han	Jiawei Han is a renowned computer scientist who specializes in research on Data Mining.
Michelin	Michelin is primarily a tire manufacturer. However, it is also famous for its Red and Green travel guides, for the Michelin stars the Red Guide awards to restaurants for their cooking, for its road maps, and for its historic emblem, the Michelin Man. It is currently the world's second largest tire manufacturer.
Wolfgang Ulaga	Wolfgang Ulaga is the Associate Professor of Marketing at the HEC School of Management. He earned a doctoral degree in marketing from the University of Paris 1, Pantheon-Sorbonne. Previously, Dr. Ulaga was a faculty member at the University of Notre Dame, ESCP-EAP and EDHEC.

58

Go to **Cram101.com** for the Practice Tests for this Chapter.

Dell	Dell develops, manufactures, sells and supports personal computers, servers, data storage devices, network switches, personal digital assistants, software, televisions, computer peripherals and other technology-related products.
Michael Dell	Michael Dell is the founder of Dell, Inc., the world's largest computer manufacturer which revolutionized the home computer industry. Michael Dell founded MSD Capital LP, a private investment firm, to invest in various small companies on his behalf. According to reports, the firm tends to invest in "late stage" investments rather than early in a company's startup.
Marketing	Marketing is the process or act of bringing together buyers and sellers. Two major factors of marketing are the recruitment of new customers and the retention and expansion of relationships with existing customers. Marketing methods are informed by many of the social sciences, particularly psychology, sociology, and economics.
Marketing strategy	A marketing strategy is a process that can allow an organization to concentrate its resources on the greatest opportunities to increase sales and achieve a sustainable competitive advantage.
Strategy	A strategy is a long term plan of action designed to achieve a particular goal, most often "winning". Strategy is differentiated from tactics or immediate actions with resources at hand by its nature of being extensively premeditated, and often practically rehearsed.
Compaq	Compaq was an American personal computer company. Compaq entered the retail computer market with the Presario, and was one of the first manufacturers in the mid-1990s to market a sub-$1000 PC. Compaq bought Tandem Computers, known for their NonStop server line. This acquisition instantly gave Compaq a presence in the higher end business computing market.
Corporation	A corporation is a legal entity which has a separate legal personality from its members. The defining legal rights and obligations of the corporation are: the ability to sue and be sued; the ability to hold assets in its own name; the ability to hire agents; the ability to sign contracts; and the ability to make by-laws, which govern its internal affairs.
Gateway	Gateway is an American computer hardware company which develops, manufactures, supports and markets a wide range of personal computers, computer monitors, servers, and computer accessories. Gateway directly and indirectly sells its products to third-party retailers, consumers, businesses, government agencies and educational institutions. The corporate structure and management of Gateway extends beyond the board of directors.
Hewlett-Packard	Hewlett-Packard is currently the world's largest information technology corporation and is known worldwide for its printers, personal computers and high end servers. The company, which once catered primarily to engineering and medical markets—a line of business it spun off as Agilent Technologies in 1999 now markets to households and small business. It is acknowledged by Wired magazine as the producer of the world's first personal computer, in 1968, the Hewlett-Packard 9100A.
IBM	IBM is a multinational computer technology and consulting corporation. It manufactures and sells computer hardware, software, infrastructure services, hosting services and consulting services in areas ranging from mainframe computers to nanotechnology.
Lenovo	Lenovo is China's largest and the world's fourth largest personal computer manufacturer, after Hewlett-Packard and Dell of the U.S. and Acer of Taiwan. Lenovo also provides information technology integration and support services, and its QDI unit offers contract manufacturing. Lenovo purchased IBM's PC Division which transformed it into a major international personal computer manufacturer. As a result of the acquisition, Lenovo gained the rights to the product lines as well as licensed trademarks.
Wal-Mart	Wal-Mart is an American public corporation, currently the world's 2nd largest corporation

Go to **Cram101.com** for the Practice Tests for this Chapter.

according to the 2007 Fortune 500. It was founded by Sam Walton in 1962.

Airline
An airline provides air transport services for passengers or freight, generally with a recognized operating certificate or license. An Airline will lease or own their aircraft with which to supply these services and may form partnerships or alliances with other airline companies for mutual benefit.

Cray
Cray Inc. is a supercomputer manufacturer founded in 1972 by computer designer Seymour Cray. Already a legend in his field by this time, Cray put his company on the map in 1976 with the release of the Cray-1 vector computer

NCR Corporation
NCR Corporation is a technology company specializing in products for the retail and financial sectors. Its main products are point-of-sale terminals, automatic teller machines, check processing systems, barcode scanners, and business consumables.

Research
Research is a human activity based on intellectual investigation and aimed at discovering, interpreting, and revising human knowledge on different aspects of the world. Research can use the scientific method, but need not do so.

Southwest Airlines
Southwest Airlines is a low-fare airline in the United States. It is the largest airline in the United States by number of passengers carried domestically for any one year and the second largest airline in the world by number of passengers carried. Southwest Airlines is one of the world's most profitable airlines and in January 2007, posted a profit for the 34th consecutive year. Its reputation for low prices and a laid-back atmosphere have made it an icon of pop culture.

US Airways
US Airways is an American airline headquartered in Tempe, Arizona, owned by US Airways Group, Inc. The airline is the sixth largest airline in the United States, and the largest low-cost airline in the United States by number of destinations.

Market
A market is, as defined in economics, a social arrangement that allows buyers and sellers to discover information and carry out a voluntary exchange of goods or services.

Igor Ansoff
Igor Ansoff was an applied mathematician and business manager. He is known as the father of Strategic management.

Cintas
Cintas operates more than 400 facilties throughout North America and provides highly specialized services to businesses, including the design and manufacturing of corporate identity uniform programs, entrance mats, restroom supplies, promotional products, first aid and safety products, fire protection services and document management services to approximately 800,000 businesses.

Diversification
Diversification in finance involves spreading investments around into many types of investments, including stocks, mutual funds, bonds, and cash. It reduces the risk of a portfolio. It does not necessarily reduce the returns. This is why diversification is referred to as the only free lunch in finance.

DuPont
DuPont is an American chemical company that is currently the world's second largest chemical company in terms of market capitalization and fourth in revenue.

Du Pont family
The Du Pont family is an American family descended from Pierre Samuel du Pont de Nemours. The son of a Paris watchmaker and a member of a Burgundian noble family, he and his sons, Victor Marie du Pont and Eleuthère Irénée du Pont, emigrated to the United States in 1800 and used the resources of this heritage to found one of the most prominent of American families, and one of its most successful corporations, E. I. du Pont de Nemours and Company,

Hertz
Hertz is the world's second largest car rental company, with 1,900 locations in the United States and 5,100 worldwide. It was a wholly owned subsidiary of Ford Motor Company. Every modern Hertz commercial features a Ford Taurus. Hertz debuted the "Prestige Collection" at

many rental locations. This collection features cars from Ford's Premier Automotive Group, including specific reservable models from Volvo, Land Rover and Jaguar.

Market development	A market development strategy targets non-buying customers in currently targeted segments. It also targets new customers in new segments.
Market penetration	Market penetration is a growth strategy when a company enters/penetrates a market with current products. The best way to achieve this is by gaining competitors' customers. Other ways include attracting non-users or convincing current clients to use more of your product/service.
Product development	In business and engineering, product development is the term used to describe the complete process of bringing a new product or service to market. Companies typically see it as the first stage in generating and commercializing new products within the overall strategic process of product life cycle management used to maintain or grow their market share.
Nissan	Nissan is Japan's second largest car company after Toyota. Nissan is among the top three Asian rivals of the "big three" in the US.
Goal setting	In business, goal setting has the advantages of encouraging participants to put in substantial effort; and, because every member is aware of what is expected of him or her, little room is left for inadequate effort going unnoticed.
Plan	Informal or ad-hoc plan are created by individuals in all of their pursuits. Structured and formal plans, used by multiple people, are more likely to occur in projects, diplomacy, careers, economic development, military campaigns, combat, or in the conduct of other business.
Renault	Renault is a French vehicle manufacturer producing cars, vans, buses, tractors, and trucks. The company is well known for numerous revolutionary designs, security technologies, and motor racing. In the twenty-first century, Renault was to foster a reputation for distinctive, outlandish design. It signed an alliance with Nissan, it is the first of its kind involving a Japanese and a French company, each with its own distinct corporate culture and brand identity, linked through cross-shareholding.
Staples	Staples is the world's largest office supply retail store chain, with over 1,700 stores worldwide. Staples and Office Depot announced plans to merge. The Federal Trade Commission decided that the superpower would unfairly increase office supply prices despite competition from the third-in-line, which did not have stores in many of the local markets that the merger would affect.
American Express	American Express is a diversified global financial services company. American Express became one of the monopolies that President Theodore Roosevelt had the Interstate Commerce Commission investigate during his administration. American Express acquired the investment banking and trading firm, Lehman Brothers Kuhn Loeb, and added it to the Shearson family, creating Shearson Lehman/American Express.
Hotel	A hotel is an establishment that provides paid lodging, usually on a short-term basis. It often provides a number of additional guest services such as a restaurant, a swimming pool or childcare. Some establishments have conference services and meeting rooms and encourage groups to hold conventions and meetings at their location.
International Paper	International Paper is an American pulp and paper company, the second largest pulp and paper company in the world. It was the largest producer of plastic lids and cups, manufacturing for the fast-food giants McDonalds, Wendys, and Subway.
Omni Hotels	Omni Hotels is a privately owned upscale hotel company based in Irving, Texas. Omni currently owns and/or manages 36 properties of which 4 are resorts.

Go to **Cram101.com** for the Practice Tests for this Chapter.

Resource allocation	Resource allocation refers to the manner in which an economy distributes its resources among the potential uses so as to produce a particular set of final goods.
Synergy	Synergy refers to the phenomenon in which two or more discrete influences or agents acting together create an effect greater than that predicted by knowing only the separate effects of the individual agents.
David Aaker	David Aaker is a brand consultant, CEO of Prophet consultancy and author of 12 books.
Analysis	Analysis means literally to break a complex problem down into smaller, more manageable "independent" parts for the purposes of examination — with the hope that solving these smaller parts will lead to a solution of the more complex problem as well.
Situation analysis	Situation analysis is a marketing term, and involves evaluating the situation and trends in a particular company's market.
SWOT	SWOT analysis, is a strategic planning tool. It involves specifying the objective of the business venture or project and identifying the internal and external factors that are favorable and unfavorable to achieving that objective. The usefulness of SWOT analysis is not limited to profit-seeking organizations. SWOT analysis may be used in any decision-making situation when a desired end-state has been defined.
Christopher Meyer	Sir Christopher Meyer, KCMG is a former British Ambassador to the United States, and the current chair of the Press Complaints Commission.
Cargill	Cargill, Incorporated is a privately held, multinational corporation, and is based in the state of Minnesota in the United States. It was founded in 1865, and has grown into the world's second largest privately held corporation.
Concept map	A concept map is a diagram showing the relationships among concepts. Concepts are connected with labelled arrows, in a downward-branching hierarchical structure. The relationship between concepts is articulated in linking phrases, e.g., "gives rise to", "results in", "is required by," or "contributes to".
Competition	Competition is a rivalry between individuals, groups, or nations for territory or resources. It arises whenever two or more parties strive for a goal that cannot be shared. Competition occurs naturally between living organisms which coexist in the same environment. For example, animals compete over water supplies, food, and mates. In addition, humans compete for attention, wealth, prestige, and fame.
Context	Context analysis, is a method to analyze the environment in which a business operates. Context analysis considers the entire environment of a business, its internal and external environment. This is an important aspect of business planning.
Porter 5 forces analysis	Porter 5 forces analysis uses concepts developed in IO economics to derive 5 forces that determine the attractiveness of a market. Michael Porter referred to these forces as the microenvironment, to contrast it with the more general term macroenvironment. They consist of those forces close to a company that affect its ability to serve its customers and make a profit.
Competitiveness	Competitiveness is a comparative concept of the ability and performance of a firm, sub-sector or country to sell and supply goods and/or services in a given market. The term may also be applied to markets, where it is used to refer to the extent to which the market structure may be regarded as perfectly competitive.
Industry	Industry, is the segment of economy concerned with production of goods. Industry began in its present form during the 1800s, aided by technological advances, and it has continued to develop to this day.
Advanced Micro	Advanced Micro Devices is an American multinational semiconductor company based in Sunnyvale,

Devices	California, that develops computer processors and related technologies for commercial and consumer markets. Its main products include microprocessors, motherboard chipsets, embedded processors and graphics processors for servers, workstations and personal computers, and processor technologies for handheld devices, digital television, and game consoles.
Intel	Intel is the world's largest semiconductor company and the inventor of the x86 series of microprocessors, the processors found in many personal computers. After 2000, growth in demand for high-end microprocessors slowed and competitors garnered significant market share, initially in low-end and mid-range processors but ultimately across the product range, and it's dominant position was reduced. Intel has become one of the world's most recognizable computer brands following its long-running "Intel Inside" campaign.
Samsung	On November 30, 2005 Samsung pleaded guilty to a charge it participated in a worldwide DRAM price fixing conspiracy during 1999-2002 that damaged competition and raized PC prices.
Red Adair	Red Adair was a renowned American oil field firefighter. He became world famous as an innovator in the highly specialized and extremely hazardous profession of extinguishing and capping blazing, erupting oil wells, both land-based and offshore.
Distribution	Distribution is one of the 4 aspects of marketing. Traditionally, distribution has been seen as dealing with logistics: how to get the product or service to the customer. There have also been some innovations in the distribution of services. For example, there has been an increase in franchizing and in rental services - the latter offering anything from televisions through tools.
Channel conflict	Channel conflict occurs when manufacturers disintermediate their channel partners, such as distributors, retailers, dealers, and sales representatives, by selling their products direct to consumers through general marketing methods and/or over the internet through eCommerce. It can also occur when there has been over production. This results in a surplus of products in the market place.
Conoco	Conoco was an American oil company founded as the Continental Oil and Transportation Company. Based in Ogden, Utah, the company was a coal, oil, kerosene, grease and candles distributor in the West. Seagram Company Ltd. engineered a takeover of Conoco. Although Seagram acquired a 32.2% stake in Conoco, DuPont was brought in as a white knight by the oil company and entered the bidding war. In the end, Seagram lost out in the Conoco bidding war.
Five competitive forces	There are five competitive forces which can be used to estimate the attractiveness and profitability of entering a business market. They consist of the threat of new entrants, competitive rivalry, the threat of substitute products, the power of buyers, and the power of suppliers
Management	Management comprises directing and controlling a group of one or more people or entities for the purpose of coordinating and harmonizing that group towards accomplishing a goal. Management often encompasses the deployment and manipulation of human resources, financial resources, technological resources, and natural resources.
Swiss Army knife	A Swiss Army knife, is a brand of multi-function pocket knife or multitool. Generally speaking, a Swiss Army knife has a blade as well as various tools, such as screwdrivers and can openers. These attachments are stowed inside the handle of the knife through a pivot point mechanism. The handle is usually red, and features a Cross and Shield, usually featuring a white cross, the emblem of Switzerland.
Komatsu	Komatsu is a Japanese company that manufactures construction and mining equipment, industry machinery such as press machines, lasers, and thermoelectric modules. Komatsu began exporting its products in the 1960s, looking to counteract the postwar image of Japanese products as being cheap and poorly made, and entered the U.S. market in July 1967, taking on Caterpillar, the world's largest bulldozer maker, in its home market.

Market orientation	Market orientation refers to the implementation of the marketing concept. It is is defined by two key characteristics: 1) the nature of the information that is collected, and 2) what business enterprises do with that information.
Organizational learning	Organizational learning is an area of knowledge within organizational theory that studies models and theories about the way an organization learns and adapts.
Pythagoras	Pythagoras was an Ionian Greek mathematician and founder of the religious movement called Pythagoreanism. He is often revered as a great mathematician, mystic and scientist; however some have questioned the scope of his contributions to mathematics and natural philosophy.
Learning	Learning is the acquisition and development of memories and behaviors, including skills, knowledge, understanding, values, and wisdom. It is the goal of education, and the product of experience.
Boeing	Boeing is the world's largest aircraft manufacturer by revenue. Headquartered in Chicago, Illinois, Boeing is the second-largest defense contractor in the world. In 2005, the company was the world's largest civil aircraft manufacturer in terms of value.
Hernan Cortes	Hernan Cortes was a Spanish conquistador who initiated the conquest of the Aztec Empire on behalf of Charles V, King of Castile and Holy Roman Emperor, in the early 16th century. Cortés was part of the generation of Spanish colonizers that began the first phase of the Spanish colonization of the Americas.
Leadership	Some commentators link leadership closely with the idea of management. Some regard the two as synonymous, and others consider management a subset of leadership. This would allow for a reciprocal relationship between leadership and management, implying that an effective manager should possess leadership skills, and an effective leader should demonstrate management skills.
Ronald Reagan	Ronald Reagan was the 40th President of the United States and the 33rd Governor of California. As president, Reagan implemented new political initiatives as well as economic policies, advocating a laissez-faire philosophy, but the extent to which these ideas were implemented is debatable.
Jack Welch	In 1986, GE acquired NBC. During the 90s, Jack Welch helped to modernize GE by emphasizing a shift from manufacturing to services. He also made hundreds of acquisitions and made a push to dominate markets abroad. Welch adopted the Six Sigma quality program in late 1995.
Delta Airlines	Delta Airlines is a major American airline headquartered in Atlanta, Georgia that operates an expansive domestic and international network. It is the sixth-largest airline in the world. It filed for Chapter 11 bankruptcy protection for the first time in its 76-year history. The company cited high labor costs and record-breaking jet fuel prices as factors in its filing. At the time of the filing, it had $20.5 billion in debt, $10 billion of which accumulated since January 2001.
Richard Farmer	Richard Farmer is an American businessman whose fortune is self-made through his development of the Cintas Corporation. The company started out as his grandfather's industrial rag cleaning business but today is the nation's leading corporate uniform provider company in the nation.
John Lehman	John Lehman is an American investment banker and writer who served as Secretary of the Navy in the Reagan administration and since 2003 has been a member of the 9/11 Commission.
Quality	In everyday language, business, engineering and manufacturing, quality consists of the characteristics of a product or service that bear on its ability to satisfy stated or implied needs; a product or service free of deficiencies.
Xerox	Xerox Corporation is a global document management company, which manufactures and sells a

Go to **Cram101.com** for the Practice Tests for this Chapter.

	range of color and black-and-white printers, multifunction systems, photo copiers, digital production printing presses, and related consulting services and supplies.
Kevin Rollins	Kevin Rollins is an American businessman and philanthropist. The former President and CEO of Dell Computers, in 2006 Rollins was named by London's CBR as the 9th Most Influential person in the Enterprise IT sector.[1]
Value	Value of a product within the context of marketing means the relationship between the consumer's expectations of product quality to the actual amount paid for it. It can be defined by both qualitative and quantitative measures. On the qualitative side, value is the perceived gain composed of individual's emotional, mental and physical condition plus various social, economic, cultural and environmental factors. On the quantitative side, value is the actual gain measured in terms of financial numbers, percentages, and dollars.
Value system	A value system refers to how an individual or a group of individuals organize their ethical or ideological values. A well-defined value system is a moral code.
Information	Information is the result of processing, gathering, manipulating and organizing data in a way that adds to the knowledge of the receiver. In other words, it is the context in which data is taken.
System	System is a set of interacting or interdependent entities, real or abstract, forming an integrated whole.
Ariba	Ariba is software and information technology services company founded on the idea of using the Internet to enable companies to facilitate and improve the procurement process.
Thomas Alva Edison	Thomas Alva Edison was an American inventor and businessman who developed many devices that greatly influenced life around the world, including the phonograph and a long lasting light bulb. Edison is considered one of the most prolific inventors in history, holding 1,093 U.S. patents in his name, as well as many patents in the United Kingdom, France and Germany.
Emerging Markets	The term emerging markets is commonly used to describe business and market activity in industrializing or emerging regions of the world. It is sometimes loosely used as a replacement for emerging economies, but really signifies a business phenomenon that is not fully described by or constrained to geography or economic strength; such countries are considered to be in a transitional phase between developing and developed status.
Power	Much of the recent sociological debate on power revolves around the issue of the enabling nature of power.
George S. Day	George S. Day is the Professor of Marketing at the Wharton School of Business, Pennsylvania, USA. His primary areas of activity are marketing, the management of new product development, strategic planning, organizational change and competitive strategies in global markets.
John Deighton	John Deighton was a Canadian bar owner who was born in Hull, England. The Gastown neighborhood of Vancouver, British Columbia is named after him.
Shelby D. Hunt	Shelby D. Hunt is the Jerry S. Rawls and P. W. Horn Professor of Marketing. He was previously an editor for the Journal of Marketing from 1984-1987, and a chairman of the Marketing Department at the University of Wisconsin-Madison from 1974-1980.
Das Narayandas	Das Narayandas is the James J. Hill Professor of Business Administration at Harvard Business School. He is the current co-chair of HBS's Program for Leadership Development. His credentials include a Bachelor of Technology degree in Engineering from the Indian Institute of Technology, a Ph.D. in Management from Purdue University, and a Post-Graduate Diploma in Management from his studies at the Indian Institute of Management.
Coimbatore Krishnarao	Coimbatore Krishnarao Prahalad is a management consultant, author, and the Paul and Ruth McCracken Distinguished University Professor of Corporate Strategy at the University of

Prahalad	Michigan Ross School of Business. He was co-founder and became CEO of Praja Inc. The goals of the company ranged from allowing common people to access information without restriction to providing a testbed for various management ideas.
Adrian Slywotzky	Adrian Slywotzky is a Managing Director of Oliver Wyman, author of the book Value Migration: How to Think Several Moves Ahead of the Competition about Marketing strategy

Cobham plc	Cobham plc is a British manufacturing company based in Wimborne Minster, Dorset, England. It is listed on the London Stock Exchange and is a constituent of the FTSE 100 Index.
Corporation	A corporation is a legal entity which has a separate legal personality from its members. The defining legal rights and obligations of the corporation are: the ability to sue and be sued; the ability to hold assets in its own name; the ability to hire agents; the ability to sign
Eaton Corporation	Eaton Corporation is a diversified industrial manufacturer with 2007 sales of $13.0 billion, putting it at 198 on the Fortune 500 for 2007. Eaton is a global leader in electrical systems and components for power quality, distribution and control; fluid power systems and services for industrial, mobile and aircraft equipment; intelligent truck drivetrain systems for safety and fuel economy; and automotive engine air management systems, powertrain solutions
Perkin-Elmer	Perkin-Elmer is an American multinational technology corporation, focused in the business areas of: Life and Analytical Sciences, Optoelectronics, and Fluid Sciences. The Perkin-Elmer Life and Analytical Sciences division engineers and manufactures drug research and development tools, chemical and environmental monitoring equipment, medical imaging devices, and genetic screening tools.
Sikorsky	Sikorsky is an American aircraft manufacturer.
Church	A church is an association of people with a common belief system, especially one that is based on the teachings of Jesus of Nazareth.
Culture	Culture generally refers to patterns of human activity and the symbolic structures that give such activities significance and importance. Different definitions of "culture" reflect different theoretical bases for understanding, or criteria for evaluating, human activity.
Organizational culture	Organizational culture comprises the attitudes, experiences, beliefs, and values of an organization.
Market	A market is, as defined in economics, a social arrangement that allows buyers and sellers to discover information and carry out a voluntary exchange of goods or services.
Market orientation	Market orientation refers to the implementation of the marketing concept. It is is defined by two key characteristics: 1) the nature of the information that is collected, and 2) what business enterprises do with that information.
Southern Baptist Convention	The Southern Baptist Convention is a United States-based Christian denomination that consists of numerous agencies, including six seminaries, two mission boards and a variety of other organizations such as: the Executive Committee of the Southern Baptist Convention, which can act for the SBC ad interim between annual meetings; Ethics & Religious Liberties Commission, Southern Baptist Foundation, and GuideStone Financial Resources.
Performance	A performance generally comprises an event in which one group of people behave in a particular way for another group of people.
Ashland	Ashland is a Fortune 500 company which operates in more than 100 countries throughout the world. Presently based in Covington, Kentucky, in the USA, the company traces its roots back to Ashland, Kentucky. On July 11, 2008, Ashland agreed to purchase another U.S. chemical company Hercules Inc. for an estimated $3.3 billion.
George S. Day	George S. Day is the Professor of Marketing at the Wharton School of Business, Pennsylvania, USA. His primary areas of activity are marketing, the management of new product development, strategic planning, organizational change and competitive strategies in global markets.
Autodesk	Autodesk is an American software and services company for the manufacturing, infrastructure, building, media and entertainment, and wireless data services fields. Autodesk was founded by John Walker and twelve other co-founders in 1982. Over its history, it has had various locations in Marin County, California, USA. It is currently headquartered in San Rafael,

Go to **Cram101.com** for the Practice Tests for this Chapter.

	California.
DHL	DHL is a Deutsche Post World Net company of Germany that provides international Mail, Express, Logistics and Finance. The company was founded in 1969 by Adrian Dalsey, Larry Hillblom, and Robert Lynn.
Quality	In everyday language, business, engineering and manufacturing, quality consists of the characteristics of a product or service that bear on its ability to satisfy stated or implied needs; a product or service free of deficiencies.
Partnership	A partnership is a type of business entity in which partners share with each other the profits or losses of the business undertaking in which all have invested.
Strategic decisions	Strategic decisions are a set of critical decisions that determine the tone and direction for the product launch, typically including platform strategies and driving strategies. Strategic decisions encompass all aspects of a selling strategy to penetrate new markets, set trends, define product/service functions, etc.
Manufacturing	Manufacturing is the use of tools and labor to make things for use or sale. The term may refer to a vast range of human activity, from handicraft to high tech, but is most commonly applied to industrial production, in which raw materials are transformed into finished goods on a large scale.
Stock	In financial terminology, stock is the capital raized by a corporation, through the issuance and sale of shares.
Dell	Dell develops, manufactures, sells and supports personal computers, servers, data storage devices, network switches, personal digital assistants, software, televisions, computer peripherals and other technology-related products.
Build to order	Build to order is a production approach where products are built after a confirmed order is received for it. It is the oldest style of order fulfillment and is still the most appropriate approach used for highly customised or low-volume products.
Unisys	Unisys Corporation, based in Blue Bell, Pennsylvania, United States, and incorporated in Delaware, is a global provider of information technology services and solutions.
Purchasing	Purchasing refers to a business or organization attempting to acquire goods or services to accomplish the goals of the enterprise. Though there are several organizations that attempt to set standards in the purchasing process, processes can vary greatly between organizations.
Marketing	Marketing is the process or act of bringing together buyers and sellers. Two major factors of marketing are the recruitment of new customers and the retention and expansion of relationships with existing customers. Marketing methods are informed by many of the social sciences, particularly psychology, sociology, and economics.
Decision	A decision is a final product of a specific mental/cognitive process by an individual or group, which is called decision making, or in more detail, Inactive decision making, Reactive decision making, and Proactive decision making. Therefore it is a subjective concept. It is a mental object and can be an opinion, a rule or a task for execution/application.
Decision making	Decision making is the cognitive process leading to the selection of a course of action among variations. In general, business and management systems should be set up to allow decision making at the lowest possible level. There are several models or practices of decision making for business.
Compensation	Deferred compensation is an arrangement in which a portion of an employee's income is paid out at a date after which that income is actually earned. Examples of deferred compensation include pensions, retirement plans, and stock options. The primary benefit of most deferred compensation is the deferral of tax to the dates at which the employee actually receives the

	income.
Human resources	Human Resources refers to the individuals within the firm, and to the portion of the firm's organization that deals with hiring, firing, training, and other personel issues.
Asea Brown Boveri	Asea Brown Boveri is a multinational corporation. It is one of the world's largest engineering companies. It has operations in around 100 countries, with approximately 109,000 employees. The purchase of the automation process allowed Asea Brown Boveri to become a leader in the global automation market.
Functional organization	The Functional organization is structured according to functional areas instead of product lines. The structure groups specialize in similar skills in separate units.
Honeywell	Honeywell is a major American multinational conglomerate company that produces a variety of consumer products, engineering services, and aerospace systems for a wide variety of customers, from private consumers to major corporations. Honeywell originally entered the computer business via a joint venture with Raytheon called Datamatic Corp., but soon bought out Raytheon's share and the business became a Honeywell division.
Valmet	Valmet was a Finnish state-owned company. Valmet was formed in 1951, when the state of Finland decided to group their various factories working on war reparations to the Soviet Union under one company. Valmet and the factories fused with it produce a wide array of products including paper machines, board machines, aeroplanes, automobiles, locomotives, weapons and everyday household appliances. Valmet merged with Rauma company in 1999, and the current Metso Corporation was created.
Learning	Learning is the acquisition and development of memories and behaviors, including skills, knowledge, understanding, values, and wisdom. It is the goal of education, and the product of experience.
Organizational learning	Organizational learning is an area of knowledge within organizational theory that studies models and theories about the way an organization learns and adapts.
Cognitive map	A cognitive map is a type of mental processing composed of a series of psychological transformations by which an individual can acquire, code, store, recall, and decode information about the relative locations and attributes of phenomena in their everyday or metaphorical spatial environment.
Federal Express	Federal Express is a cargo airline, printing, and courier company offering overnight courier, ground, heavy freight, document copying and logistics services.
Experiment	In the scientific method, an experiment is a set of observations performed in the context of solving a particular problem or question, to support or falsify a hypothesis or research concerning phenomena. The experiment is a cornerstone in the empirical approach to acquiring deeper knowledge about the physical world.
Motorola	Motorola is an American multinational communications company based in Schaumburg, Illinois, a Chicago suburb. Motorola developed the first truly global communication network using a set of 66 satellites. The business ambitions behind this project and the need for raising venture capital to fund the project led to the creation of the Iridium company. Recently, it has ventured off to start a wireless phone service with Bradford Mobile Phones, and Kansas City Gold.
Case study	The case study is one of several ways of doing social science research. Rather than using large samples and following a rigid protocol to examine a limited number of variables, case study methods involve an in-depth, longitudinal examination of a single instance or event: a case.
Shell	Shell is a multinational oil company of British and Dutch origins. It is one of the largest

Go to **Cram101.com** for the Practice Tests for this Chapter.

	private sector energy corporations in the world, and one of the six "supermajors".
Satyam Computers	Satyam Computers is a consulting and information technology services company based in Hyderabad, India. The company offers a variety of information technology services spanning various industry sectors, and is listed on the New York Stock Exchange.
Supply	The supply is the relationship between the quantity of goods supplied by the producers of a good and the current market price. It is graphically represented by the supply curve. It is commonly represented as directly proportional to price.
Commitment	Personal commitment is the act or quality of voluntarily taking on or fulfilling obligations. What makes personal commitment "personal" is the voluntary aspect. In particular, it is not necessary that a personal commitment relate to personal interests.
Planning	Planning is both the organizational process of creating and maintaining a plan; and the psychological process of thinking about the activities required to create a desired future on some scale.
Active listening	Active listening is an intent to "listen for meaning", in which the listener checks with the speaker to see that a statement has been correctly heard and understood. Active listening is used in a wide variety of situations, including interviews in employment, counseling and journalistic settings.
Negotiation	Negotiation is the process whereby interested parties resolve disputes, agree upon courses of action, bargain for individual or collective advantage, and/or attempt to craft outcomes which serve their mutual interests.
Campbell	Campbell Soup Company is a well-known American producer of canned soups and related products. Campbell's products are sold in 120 countries around the world. It is headquartered in Camden, New Jersey. The company reportedly produces almost 2.5 billion cans of soup per year
Ian Chaston	Ian Chaston is the Professor of Marketing and Entrepreneurship and Director of the Management Center at Plymouth Business School. He is also an accomplished author on the subjects of management and marketing, as noted in his books Entrepreneurial Marketing: Successfully Challenging Market Convention, Managerial Effectiveness in Fisheries and Aquaculture, and Knowledge-Based Marketing: The Twenty-First Century Competitive Edge. He is also known for developing an extensive set of power-point slides that are used by lecturers to support their seminars by providing extensive, detailed information.
Bond	A bond is a debt security, in which the authorized issuer owes the holders a debt and is obliged to repay the principal and interest at a later date, termed maturity. A bond is simply a loan, but in the form of a security, although terminology used is rather different. The issuer is equivalent to the borrower, the bond holder to the lender, and the coupon to the interest.
Gregory S. Carpenter	Gregory S. Carpenter is a Professor of Marketing Strategy at the Kellogg Business School, providing instruction in masters, doctoral, and executive programs. Professor Carpenter was voted Outstanding Professor of the Year by the Kellogg Managers' Program in 1992, and received the Sidney J. Levy Teaching Award in 1996. He was recognized by the journal BusinessWeek as an outstanding faculty in its Guide to the Best Business Schools.

IBM	IBM is a multinational computer technology and consulting corporation. It manufactures and sells computer hardware, software, infrastructure services, hosting services and consulting services in areas ranging from mainframe computers to nanotechnology.
Joseph M. Tucci	Joseph M. Tucci is Chairman of the Board of Directors, President and Chief Executive Officer of EMC Corporation. Tucci has been EMC's Chairman since January 2006 and President and CEO since January 2001, one year after he joined the company as President and Chief Operating Officer.
Benefits	Employee benefits are various non-wage compensations provided to employees in addition to their normal wages or salaries. Where an employee exchanges cash wages for some other form of benefit, this is generally referred to as a 'salary sacrifice' arrangement. In most countries, most kinds of employee benefits are taxable to at least some degree.
Corporation	A corporation is a legal entity which has a separate legal personality from its members. The defining legal rights and obligations of the corporation are: the ability to sue and be sued; the ability to hold assets in its own name; the ability to hire agents; the ability to sign contracts; and the ability to make by-laws, which govern its internal affairs.
Dell	Dell develops, manufactures, sells and supports personal computers, servers, data storage devices, network switches, personal digital assistants, software, televisions, computer peripherals and other technology-related products.
Service	In economics and marketing, a service is the non-material equivalent of a good. Service has been defined as an economic activity that does not result in ownership, and this is what differentiates it from providing physical goods.
Logic	Logic is the study of the principles of valid inference and demonstration.
Accenture	Accenture Ltd. is a global management consulting, technology services, and outsourcing company with its main business office in Chicago, Illinois. It is the largest consulting firm in the world and is one of the largest computer services and software companies on the Fortune Global 500 list.
Canon	Canon is a Japanese company that specializes in imaging and optical products, including cameras, photocopiers and computer printers. Despite the company's high profile in the consumer market for cameras and computer printers, most of the company revenue comes from the office products division.
Honda	Honda is a Japanese multinational corporation, engine manufacturer and engineering corporation. Honda is the largest engine-maker in the world, producing more than 14 million internal combustion engines built each year. It was the first Japanese automaker to introduce a separate luxury line of vehicles. Many of it's most remarkable advertising campaigns have been released for the UK market, and have not been broadcast in North America except on the
Product life cycle	The Product life cycle refers to the succession of stages a product goes through. It goes through many phases and involves many professional disciplines and requires many skills, tools, processes. Product life cycle is to do with the life of a product in the market with respect to business/commercial costs and sales measures.
Product line	A group of products that are physically similar or are intended for a similar market are called the product line.
Technology	Technology is a broad concept that deals with a species' usage and knowledge of tools and crafts, and how it affects a species' ability to control and adapt to its environment. In human society, it is a consequence of science and engineering, although several technological advances predate the two concepts.
Management	Management comprises directing and controlling a group of one or more people or entities for

Go to **Cram101.com** for the Practice Tests for this Chapter.

Chapter 8. Developing and Managing Offerings: What Do Customers Want?

the purpose of coordinating and harmonizing that group towards accomplishing a goal. Management often encompasses the deployment and manipulation of human resources, financial resources, technological resources, and natural resources.

Platform

In computing, a platform describes some sort of hardware architecture or software framework, that allows software to run. Typical platforms include a computer's architecture, operating system, programming languages and related runtime libraries or graphical user interface.

Leapfrogging

Leapfrogging is a theory of development in which developing countries skip inferior, less efficient, more expensive or more polluting technologies and industries and move directly to more advanced ones.

Xerox

Xerox Corporation is a global document management company, which manufactures and sells a range of color and black-and-white printers, multifunction systems, photo copiers, digital production printing presses, and related consulting services and supplies.

Developing product solutions

Developing product solutions consists of the many strategies and tactics used to advertise future products and make them available to the public.

Strategy

A strategy is a long term plan of action designed to achieve a particular goal, most often "winning". Strategy is differentiated from tactics or immediate actions with resources at hand by its nature of being extensively premeditated, and often practically rehearsed.

Boston Consulting Group

The Boston Consulting Group is a management consulting firm founded by Harvard Business School alum Bruce Henderson in 1963. In 1965 Bruce Henderson thought that to survive, much less grow, in a competitive landscape occupied by hundreds of larger and better-known consulting firms, a distinctive identity was needed, and pioneered "Business Strategy" as a special area of expertise.

Growth

Growth refers to an increase in some quantity over time. The quantity can be physical or abstract. It can also refer to the mode of growth, i.e. numeric models for describing how much a particular quantity grows over time:

Maturity

Maturity refers to the final payment date of a loan or other financial instrument, after which point no further interest or principal need be paid.

Primary demand

Primary demand refers to desire for the product class rather than for a specific brand.

Demand

The demand represents the amount of a good that buyers are willing and able to purchase at various prices, assuming all other non-price factors remain the same. The demand curve is almost always represented as downwards-sloping, meaning that as price decreases, consumers will buy more of the good.

Portfolio

In finance, a portfolio is an appropriate mix of or collection of investments held by an institution or a private individual. In building up an investment portfolio a financial institution will typically conduct its own investment analysis, whilst a private individual may make use of the services of a financial advisor or a financial institution which offers portfolio management services.

Business strength

Business strength is the ability of an enterprise to penetrate new markets sucessfully and to be able to have the financial capability and clout to determine the terms of negotiation with other smaller companies. The greater the strength of the business - the more bargaining power that enterprise possesses to decide its own terms in contract negotiations and the marketplace.

Cash

Cash usually refers to money in the form of currency, such as banknotes and coins.

Cash cow

A cash cow is a product or a business unit that generates unusually high profit margins: so high that it is responsible for a large amount of a company's operating profit. This

Go to **Cram101.com** for the Practice Tests for this Chapter.

profit far exceeds the amount necessary to maintain the cash cow business, and the excess is used by the business for other purposes.

Digital on-screen graphic	A Digital on-screen graphic is a watermark-like station logo that many television broadcasters overlay over a portion of the screen-area of their programs to assist viewers in identifying the channel.
Market	A market is, as defined in economics, a social arrangement that allows buyers and sellers to discover information and carry out a voluntary exchange of goods or services.
Question mark	The question mark is a punctuation mark that replaces the full stop at the end of an interrogative sentence. It is also often used in place of missing or unknown data.
Star	A star is often used as a symbol for classification purposes. It is used by reviewers for ranking things such as movies, TV shows, restaurants, and hotels.
DuPont	DuPont is an American chemical company that is currently the world's second largest chemical company in terms of market capitalization and fourth in revenue.
Du Pont family	The Du Pont family is an American family descended from Pierre Samuel du Pont de Nemours. The son of a Paris watchmaker and a member of a Burgundian noble family, he and his sons, Victor Marie du Pont and Eleuthère Irénée du Pont, emigrated to the United States in 1800 and used the resources of this heritage to found one of the most prominent of American families, and one of its most successful corporations, E. I. du Pont de Nemours and Company,
Investment	Investment refers to spending for the production and accumulation of capital and additions to inventories. In a financial sense, buying an asset with the expectation of making a return.
Investment risk	The possibility of a loss of value in investments purchased is investment risk. Depending on the nature of the investment, the type of investment risk will vary.
Market opportunity	A market opportunity emerges if a product, based on either one technology or several, fulfills the need of a market better than the competition and better than substitution-technologies within the given environmental frame.
Opportunity	A business opportunity involves the sale or lease of any product, service, equipment, etc. that will enable the purchaser-licensee to begin a business. The licensor or seller of a business opportunity usually declares that it will secure or assist the buyer in finding a suitable location or provide the product to the purchaser-licensee.
Bombardier	Bombardier Inc. is a Canadian conglomerate.
Idea	An idea is an image, also concept or abstraction formed and existing in the mind. Human capability to contemplate them is associated with the ability of reasoning, self-reflection, and the ability to acquire and apply intellect. Further, they give rise to actual concepts, or mind generalisations, which are the basis for any kind of knowledge whether science or philosophy.
Idea generation	Developing a pool of concepts as candidates for new products is called idea generation.
Intel	Intel is the world's largest semiconductor company and the inventor of the x86 series of microprocessors, the processors found in many personal computers. After 2000, growth in demand for high-end microprocessors slowed and competitors garnered significant market share, initially in low-end and mid-range processors but ultimately across the product range, and it's dominant position was reduced. Intel has become one of the world's most recognizable computer brands following its long-running "Intel Inside" campaign.
Kodak	Kodak is an American multinational public company that produces photographic materials and equipment. It is known for digital photography, health imaging, and printing. The company was founded in 1892 by George Eastman.

Chapter 8. Developing and Managing Offerings: What Do Customers Want?

Motorola	Motorola is an American multinational communications company based in Schaumburg, Illinois, a Chicago suburb. Motorola developed the first truly global communication network using a set of 66 satellites. The business ambitions behind this project and the need for raising venture capital to fund the project led to the creation of the Iridium company. Recently, it has ventured off to start a wireless phone service with Bradford Mobile Phones, and Kansas City Gold.
Generation	Generation, also known as procreation, is the act of producing offspring. It can also refer to the act of creating something inanimate such as electrical generation or cryptographic code generation..
Bank	A bank is a financial institution that acts as a payment agent for customers, and borrows and lends money. In some countries such as Germany and Japan banks are the primary owners of industrial corporations while in other countries such as the United States banks are prohibited from owning non-financial companies.
Diamond	Diamond is the hardest known natural material and the third-hardest known material after aggregated diamond nanorods and ultrahard fullerite. Its hardness and high dispersion of light make it useful for industrial applications and jewelry. About 130 million carats (26,000 kg) are mined annually, with a total value of nearly USD $9 billion.
Valero Energy Corporation	Valero Energy Corporation owns and operates 17 refineries throughout the United States, Canada and the Caribbean with a combined throughput capacity of approximately 3.3 million barrels per day, making it the largest refiner in North America
Lead user	A lead user is an user of a product that currently experience needs still unknown to the public and who also benefit greatly if they obtain a solution to these needs.
United States Army Signal Corps	The United States Army Signal Corps develops, tests, provides, and manages communications and information systems support for the command and control of combined arms forces. It was founded in 1860 by United States Army Major Albert J. Myer, a physician by training, and has had an important role from the American Civil War through the current day. Over its history, it had the initial responsibility for a number of functions and new technologies that are currently managed by other organizations, including military intelligence, weather forecasting, and aviation.
Users	Users refer to people in the organization who actually use the product or service purchased by the buying center.
Nortel	Nortel is a multinational telecommunications equipment manufacturer headquartered in Toronto, Canada. This company was incorporated as the Northern Electric and Manufacturing Company Limited. Nortel is a long established industry leader in delivering end-to-end carrier grade telecommunications network infrastructure and solutions. The company has decades of experience in delivering robust, fault tolerant, software architectures and the know-how to scale to millions of users and manage thousands of network elements.
Screening	Screening in economics refers to a strategy of combating adverse selection, one of the potential decision-making complications in cases of asymmetric information.
Cordis	Cordis is a medical device company owned by Johnson & Johnson. The company was founded in Miami in 1959 and is currently headquartered in Warren, New Jersey.
Quality	In everyday language, business, engineering and manufacturing, quality consists of the characteristics of a product or service that bear on its ability to satisfy stated or implied needs; a product or service free of deficiencies.
Quality Function Deployment	Quality function deployment involves developing a matrix that includes customer preferences and product attributes. A quality function deployment matrix allows a firm to quantitatively analyze the relationship between customer needs and design attributes.

90

Go to **Cram101.com** for the Practice Tests for this Chapter.

Specification	A specification is an explicit set of requirements to be satisfied by a material, product, or service.
Product development	In business and engineering, product development is the term used to describe the complete process of bringing a new product or service to market. Companies typically see it as the first stage in generating and commercializing new products within the overall strategic process of product life cycle management used to maintain or grow their market share.
Applied Materials	Applied Materials, Inc. is the global leader in nanomanufacturing technology solutions with a broad portfolio of innovative equipment, service and software products for the fabrication of semiconductor chips, flat panel solar displays, solar photovoltaic cells, flexible electronics and energy efficient glass.
Early supplier involvement	Early supplier involvement is a practice which focuses on the involvement of one or more selected suppliers with the buyer's product design team early in the product development process. The overall goal is to use the supplier's expertise and experience in the development of a product specification that is designed for effective and efficient product allocation.
Materials	Materials are physical substances used as inputs to production or manufacturing. Materials range from man made synthetics such as many plastics to natural materials such as copper or wood.
Supply chain	A supply chain, logistics network, or supply network is the system of organizations, people, activities, information and resources involved in moving a product or service from suppli-er to customer. Supply chain activities transform raw materials and components into a finished product that is delivered to the end customer.
Software testing	Software testing is the process used to measure the quality of developed computer software. Usually, quality is constrained to such topics as correctness, completeness, security, but can also include more technical requirements as described under the ISO standard ISO 9126, such as capability, reliability, efficiency, portability, maintainability, compatibility, and usability.
Hewlett-Packard	Hewlett-Packard is currently the world's largest information technology corporation and is known worldwide for its printers, personal computers and high end servers. The company, which once catered primarily to engineering and medical markets—a line of business it spun off as Agilent Technologies in 1999 now markets to households and small business. It is acknowledged by Wired magazine as the producer of the world's first personal computer, in 1968, the Hewlett-Packard 9100A.
Lexmark	Lexmark is an American corporation which develops and manufactures printing and imaging solutions, including laser and inkjet printers, multifunction products, printing supplies, and services for business and individual consumers.
Evaluation	Evaluation is the systematic determination of merit, worth, and significance of something or someone. Evaluation often is used to characterize and appraise subjects of interest in a wide range of human enterprises, including the Arts, business, computer science, criminal justice, engineering, foundations and non-profit organizations, government, health care, and other human services.
First-mover advantage	First-mover advantage is the advantage gained by the initial occupant of a market segment. This advantage may stem from the fact that the first entrant can gain control of resources that followers may not be able to match.
Payback	A value that indicates the time period required to recoup an initial investment is a payback. The payback does not include the time-value-of-money concept.
Manufacturing	Manufacturing is the use of tools and labor to make things for use or sale. The term may

Chapter 8. Developing and Managing Offerings: What Do Customers Want?

refer to a vast range of human activity, from handicraft to high tech, but is most commonly applied to industrial production, in which raw materials are transformed into finished goods on a large scale.

Sunk cost	In economics and in business decision-making, a sunk cost is a cost that have been incurred and which cannot be recovered to any significant degree. They are sometimes contrasted with variable costs, which are the costs that will change due to the proposed course of action.
Cost	In economics, business, and accounting, a cost is the value of money that has been used up to produce something.
H. B. Fuller	H. B. Fuller is the second largest producer of adhesives worldwide. It not only produces adhesives, but has a specialty group, that produces for example paints and powder coatings.
Hitachi	Hitachi, Ltd is a Japanese global company headquartered in Marunouchi Itchome, Chiyoda, Tokyo, Japan. On the 2007 Forbes Global 2000 list, Hitachi is ranked number 371.
Satyam Computers	Satyam Computers is a consulting and information technology services company based in Hyderabad, India. The company offers a variety of information technology services spanning various industry sectors, and is listed on the New York Stock Exchange.
Software	Software is a general term used to describe a collection of computer programs, procedures and documentation that perform some task on a computer system.
Instrument	Instrument refers to an economic variable that is controlled by policy makers and can be used to influence other variables, called targets. Examples are monetary and fiscal policies used to achieve external and internal balance.
Siebel	Siebel is a brand name of Oracle Corporation. Siebel was the dominant Customer Relationship Management vendor in the late 1990s, peaking at 45% of the CRM market share in 2002. It had two acquisitions in September and October 1997: InterActive WorkPlace Inc., which specialized in intranet-based business intelligence software, for $15 million in stock, and Nomadic Systems Inc., which focused on the pharmaceutical industry, for $11 million in stock.
System	System is a set of interacting or interdependent entities, real or abstract, forming an integrated whole.
Texas Instruments	Texas Instruments is an American company based in Dallas, Texas, USA, renowned for developing and commercializing semiconductor and computer technology. Texas Instruments had two interesting problems with engineering and product development after the introduction of the semiconductor and the microprocessor.
Upgrade	The term upgrade is most often used in computing and consumer electronics, generally meaning a replacement of hardware, software or firmware with a newer version, in order to bring the system up to date. The word is also used by audiophiles to describe the replacement of a product with a better quality product with the aim of bringing enhancements to sound quality.
Dow Corning	Dow Corning is a multinational corporation specialized in silicon and silicone-based technology, offering more than 7,000 products and services. A large, majority-owned subsidiary of Dow Corning Corporation is the Hemlock Semiconductor Corporation. Class-action lawsuits claimed that it's silicone breast implants caused systemic health problems. The claims first centered around breast cancer, and then migrated to a range of autoimmune diseases, including lupus, rheumatoid arthritis and various neurological problems. This led to numerous lawsuits. As a result, Dow Corning was in bankruptcy protection for nine years, ending in June 2004
Innovation	An innovation must be substantially different, not an insignificant change. In economics the change must increase value, customer value, or producer value. Innovations are intended to make someone better off, and the succession of many innovations grows the whole economy.

Go to **Cram101.com** for the Practice Tests for this Chapter.

Citibank	Citibank is a major international bank and is now the consumer and corporate banking arm of financial services giant Citigroup, one of the largest companies in the world. As of March 2007, it is the largest bank in the United States by holdings.
Drucker	Drucker as a business thinker took off in the 1940s, when his initial writings on politics and society won him access to the internal workings of General Motors, which was one of the largest companies in the world at that time. His experiences in Europe had left him fascinated with the problem of authority.
Employee	An employee contributes labor and expertise to an endeavour. Employees perform the discrete activity of economic production. Of the three factors of production, employees usually provide the labor.
Human resource management	Human resource management is the strategic and coherent approach to the management of an organization's most valued assets - the people working there who individually and collectively contribute to the achievement of the objectives of the business.
Resource Management	Resource management is the efficient and effective deployment of an organization's resources when they are needed. Such resources may include financial resources, inventory, human skills, production resources, or information technology.
Orientation and training	Orientation and training is the introductory process that educates new employees to the concepts, goals, and procedures of a business and their roles within the organization.
William Boulding	William Boulding is a Professor of Marketing and Senior Associate Dean for Programs at the Duke University Fuqua School of Business. His areas of expertise include Marketing Strategy, Marketing Metrics, and Management of the Customer Asset. His teaching and research interests include Marketing Strategy, Customer Relationship Metrics, and Marketing Decision-Making. He received his Ph.D. from Wharton School, University of Pennsylvania in 1986.
Ford	Ford is an American company that manufactures and sells automobiles worldwide. Ford introduced methods for large-scale manufacturing of cars, and large-scale management of an industrial workforce, especially elaborately engineered manufacturing sequences typified by the moving assembly lines.
Eric Von Hippel	Eric von Hippel is an economist and a professor at the MIT Sloan School of Management, specializing in the nature and economics of distributed and open innovation. He is best known for his work developing the concept of user innovation – that end-users, rather than manufacturers, are responsible for a large amount of new innovation. In order to describe this phenomenon, he introduced the term lead user in 1986. His work has applications in business strategy and free/open source software.
Christian Homburg	Christian Homburg is a Professor of Business Administration at the University of Mannheim in Germany. He received his Diploma in Mathematics and Business Administration from the University of Karlsruhe and a doctorate in Business Administration also from the University of Karlsruhe.
Campbell	Campbell Soup Company is a well-known American producer of canned soups and related products. Campbell's products are sold in 120 countries around the world. It is headquartered in Camden, New Jersey. The company reportedly produces almost 2.5 billion cans of soup per year

Distribution	Distribution is one of the 4 aspects of marketing. Traditionally, distribution has been seen as dealing with logistics: how to get the product or service to the customer. There have also been some innovations in the distribution of services. For example, there has been an
Channel intermediaries	Channel intermediaries are those sources where businesses are able to purchase their products. These can include wholesalers, agents, retailers, & the Internet.
Home Depot	The Home Depot is an American retailer of home improvement and construction products and services. The Home Depot is the largest home improvement retailer and second-largest general retailer in the United States. The slogan "You can do it. We can help." has been used by the Home Depot since 2003. Home Depot and Robert Nardelli mutually agreed on Nardelli's resignation as CEO after a six-year tenure.
Cost	In economics, business, and accounting, a cost is the value of money that has been used up to produce something.
Intermediary	An intermediary is a third party that offers intermediation services between two trading parties. The intermediary acts as a conduit for goods or services offered by a supplier to a consumer.
Management	Management comprises directing and controlling a group of one or more people or entities for the purpose of coordinating and harmonizing that group towards accomplishing a goal. Management often encompasses the deployment and manipulation of human resources, financial resources, technological resources, and natural resources.
Supply	The supply is the relationship between the quantity of goods supplied by the producers of a good and the current market price. It is graphically represented by the supply curve. It is commonly represented as directly proportional to price.
Supply chain	A supply chain, logistics network, or supply network is the system of organizations, people, activities, information and resources involved in moving a product or service from suppli-er to customer. Supply chain activities transform raw materials and components into a finished product that is delivered to the end customer.
Supply chain management	Supply chain management is the process of planning, implementing, and controlling the operations of the supply chain with the purpose to satisfy customer requirements as efficiently as possible. Supply chain management spans all movement and storage of raw materials, work-in-process inventory, and finished goods from point-of-origin to point-of-consumption.
Buyer	A buyer is any person who contracts to acquire an asset in return for some form of consideration.
Closing costs	Real property in most jurisdictions is conveyed from the seller to the buyer through a real estate contract. The point in time at which the contract is actually executed and the title to the property is conveyed to the buyer is known as the "closing". It is common for a variety of costs associated with the transaction to be incurred by either the buyer or the seller. These costs are typically paid at the closing, and are known as closing costs.
Profit	Profit generally is the making of gain in business activity for the benefit of the owners of the business. The word comes from Latin meaning "to make progress", is defined in two different ways, one for economics and one for accounting.
Channel members	Channel members defined the simplest level, that of direct contact with no intermediaries involved, as the 'zero-level' channel. In small markets it is practical to reach the whole market using just one- and zero-level channels. In large markets a second level, a wholesaler for example, is now mainly used to extend distribution to the large number of small, neighborhood retailers.

Go to Cram101.com for the Practice Tests for this Chapter.

Asea Brown Boveri	Asea Brown Boveri is a multinational corporation. It is one of the world's largest engineering companies. It has operations in around 100 countries, with approximately 109,000 employees. The purchase of the automation process allowed Asea Brown Boveri to become a leader in the global automation market.
Industry	Industry, is the segment of economy concerned with production of goods. Industry began in its present form during the 1800s, aided by technological advances, and it has continued to develop to this day.
Merchant	Under the Uniform Commercial Code, one who regularly deals in goods of the kind sold in the contract at issue, or holds himself out as having special knowledge or skill relevant to such goods, or who makes the sale through an agent who regularly deals in such goods or claims such knowledge or skill is referred to as merchant.
Office Max	Office Max is an office supplies retailer founded in 1988 and headquartered in Naperville, Illinois. It is the third-largest office supplies retailer in the USA. In 1991, Kmart acquired Office Max to join its other subsidiaries, Sports Authority and Builders Square. Shortly after the acquisition Kmart merged its other subsidiary, Office Square, into Office Max. Kmart also acquired BizMart and merged it into Office Max in 1992.
Staples	Staples is the world's largest office supply retail store chain, with over 1,700 stores worldwide. Staples and Office Depot announced plans to merge. The Federal Trade Commission decided that the superpower would unfairly increase office supply prices despite competition from the third-in-line, which did not have stores in many of the local markets that the merger would affect.
Merchant wholesaler	Independently owned firms that take title to the goods they handle is a merchant wholesaler.
Sales	Sales is the act of providing a product or service in return for money or other compensation. It is an act of completion of a commercial activity.
Service	In economics and marketing, a service is the non-material equivalent of a good. Service has been defined as an economic activity that does not result in ownership, and this is what differentiates it from providing physical goods.
Wholesalers	Wholesaling is the sale of goods or merchandise to retailers, to industrial, commercial, institutional, or other professional business users, or to other wholesalers and related subordinated services.
Cash-and-carry	Cash-and-carry is a form of trade in which goods are sold from a wholesale warehouse operated either on a self-service basis, or on the basis of samples with the customer selecting from specimen articles using a manual or computerized ordering system but not serving himself or a combination of the two.
Drop shipping	Drop shipping is a supply chain management technique in which the retailer does not keep goods in stock, but instead transfers customer orders and shipment details to wholesalers, who then ship the goods directly to the customer . The retailers make their profit on the difference between the wholesale and retail price.
Wholesaling	Wholesaling is the sale of goods or merchandise to retailers, to industrial, commercial, institutional, or other professional business users, or to other wholesalers and related subordinated services.
Snap-on	Snap-on is a leading U.S. designer, manufacturer and marketer of tools and equipment to professional tool users. It was founded in 1920. Snap-on is located in Kenosha, Wisconsin, and employs approximately 11,500 people worldwide. The company is currently worth 2.4 billion dollars and is one of the companies on the S&P 500.

Truck jobber	Truck jobber refers to small merchant wholesalers who have a small warehouse from which they stock their trucks for distribution to retailers. They handle products such as bakery items, dairy products, and meat.
Jobber	A jobber is a trader whose strategy is to enter and exit trades quickly for small but frequent profit, without carrying a position overnight.
American Science and Surplus	American Science and Surplus is a seller of surplus and educational goods, many of which are odd, amusing, and/or useful. AS&S is unique among surplus retailers in that the humor contained in their catalog is a significant enticement to buy items in the catalog to continue receiving it.
Broker	A broker is a party that mediates between a buyer and a seller. A broker who also acts as a seller or as a buyer becomes a principal party to the deal.
Dow Corning	Dow Corning is a multinational corporation specialized in silicon and silicone-based technology, offering more than 7,000 products and services. A large, majority-owned subsidiary of Dow Corning Corporation is the Hemlock Semiconductor Corporation. Class-action lawsuits claimed that it's silicone breast implants caused systemic health problems. The claims first centered around breast cancer, and then migrated to a range of autoimmune diseases, including lupus, rheumatoid arthritis and various neurological problems. This led to numerous lawsuits. As a result, Dow Corning was in bankruptcy protection for nine years,
Design	Design, usually considered in the context of the applied arts, engineering, architecture, and other such creative endeavors, is used both as a noun and a verb. As a verb, "to design" refers to the process of originating and developing a plan for a product, structure, system, or component.
Index	In economics and finance, an index is a single number calculated from an array of prices or of quantities. Examples are a price index, a quantity index, a market performance Index. Values of the index in successive periods summarize level of the activity over time or across economic units.
Avnet	Avnet, Inc. is a technology B 2 B distributor headquartered in Phoenix, Arizona. Avnet, Inc., is one of the world's largest value-added distributors of semiconductors, connectors, passive and electromechanical components, and RF & microwave devices; enterprise networking and computer equipment, and embedded subsystems from leading manufacturers. Serving customers in 70 countries, Avnet markets, inventories, and adds value to these products.
Federal Express	Federal Express is a cargo airline, printing, and courier company offering overnight courier, ground, heavy freight, document copying and logistics services.
Coca-Cola	Coca-Cola is the world's most recognizable brand, according to BusinessWeek. The first serving in 1886 cost US$0.05. The Coca-Cola is the world's largest consumer of natural vanilla extract. The exact formula of Coca-Cola is a famous trade secret. The original copy of the formula is held in SunTrust Bank's main vault in Atlanta.
Gap	Gap is an American clothing and accessories retailer. The Gap continued to expand rapidly had expanded to areas outside of California and was entering the East coast market with its store in Voorhees, New Jersey. The Gap stores appeal to a broader midrange of customers. Although Gap, along with other retail-store chains, has been criticized for blandness and uniformity in its selling environments, the firm maintains that it tailors its stores "to appeal to unique markets" by developing multiple formats and designs.
Gap analysis	In business and economics, gap analysis is a business resource assessment tool enabling a company to compare its actual performance with its potential performance.
Hyundai	Hyundai refers to a group of companies and related organizations founded by Chung Ju-yung in South Korea.

Go to **Cram101.com** for the Practice Tests for this Chapter.

Analysis	Analysis means literally to break a complex problem down into smaller, more manageable "independent" parts for the purposes of examination — with the hope that solving these smaller parts will lead to a solution of the more complex problem as well.
Competition	Competition is a rivalry between individuals, groups, or nations for territory or resources. It arises whenever two or more parties strive for a goal that cannot be shared. Competition occurs naturally between living organisms which coexist in the same environment. For example, animals compete over water supplies, food, and mates. In addition, humans compete for attention, wealth, prestige, and fame.
Corporation	A corporation is a legal entity which has a separate legal personality from its members. The defining legal rights and obligations of the corporation are: the ability to sue and be sued; the ability to hold assets in its own name; the ability to hire agents; the ability to sign contracts; and the ability to make by-laws, which govern its internal affairs.
Dell	Dell develops, manufactures, sells and supports personal computers, servers, data storage devices, network switches, personal digital assistants, software, televisions, computer peripherals and other technology-related products.
Enterprise	Enterprise refers to another name for a business organization. Other similar terms are business firm, sometimes simply business, sometimes simply firm, as well as company, and entity.
Hewlett-Packard	Hewlett-Packard is currently the world's largest information technology corporation and is known worldwide for its printers, personal computers and high end servers. The company, which once catered primarily to engineering and medical markets—a line of business it spun off as Agilent Technologies in 1999 now markets to households and small business. It is acknowledged by Wired magazine as the producer of the world's first personal computer, in 1968, the Hewlett-Packard 9100A.
IBM	IBM is a multinational computer technology and consulting corporation. It manufactures and sells computer hardware, software, infrastructure services, hosting services and consulting services in areas ranging from mainframe computers to nanotechnology.
Microsoft	Microsoft is an American multinational computer technology corporation. develops, manufactures, licenses and supports a wide range of software products for computing devices. Microsoft has footholds in other markets besides operating systems and office suites, with assets such as the MSNBC cable television network, the MSN Internet portal, and the Microsoft Encarta multimedia encyclopedia. It has often been described as having a developer-centric business culture.
Layoff	A layoff is the termination of employment of an employee or a group of employees for business reasons, such as the decision that certain positions are no longer necessary. Originally the term "layoff" referred specifically to a temporary interruption in work, as when factory work cyclically falls off. However, the term has long been applied also to the permanent elimination of positions as a cost-cutting measure.
Exchange	The trade of things of value between buyer and seller so that each is better off after the trade is called the exchange.
Channel conflict	Channel conflict occurs when manufacturers disintermediate their channel partners, such as distributors, retailers, dealers, and sales representatives, by selling their products direct to consumers through general marketing methods and/or over the internet through eCommerce. It can also occur when there has been over production. This results in a surplus of products in the market place.
Goal	An objective or goal is a personal or organizational desired end point in development. It is usually endeavored to be reached in finite time by setting deadlines.

Aggression	In psychology and other social and behavioral sciences, aggression refers to behavior that is intended to cause harm or pain. Aggression can be either physical or verbal.
Power	Much of the recent sociological debate on power revolves around the issue of the enabling nature of power.
Reward	A psychological reward is a process that reinforces behavior — something that, when offered, causes a behavior to increase in intensity. Reward is an operational concept for describing the positive value an individual ascribes to an object, behavioral act or an internal physical state.
Expert	An expert is someone widely recognized as a reliable source of technique or skill whose faculty for judging or deciding rightly, justly, or wisely is accorded authority and status by their peers or the public. An expert, more generally, is a person with extensive knowledge or ability in a particular area of study.
Expert power	The extent to which a person controls information that is valuable to someone else is referred to as expert power.
Legitimacy	The word legitimacy is often interpreted in a normative or a positive way.
Legitimate power	Legitimate power refers to power that is granted by virtue of one's position in the organization.
Referent power	Referent power is individual power based on a high level of identification with, admiration of, or respect for the powerholder.
Information	Information is the result of processing, gathering, manipulating and organizing data in a way that adds to the knowledge of the receiver. In other words, it is the context in which data is taken.
Holiday Inn	Holiday Inn is a brand name applied to hotels within the InterContinental Hotels Group. Although still a healthy company, changing business conditions and demographics saw Holiday Inn lose its market dominance in the 1980s. The brand name Holiday Inn is now owned by IHG who in turn license it out to franchisees and third parties who operate hotels under management agreements.
Airline	An airline provides air transport services for passengers or freight, generally with a recognized operating certificate or license. An Airline will lease or own their aircraft with which to supply these services and may form partnerships or alliances with other airline companies for mutual benefit.
American Airlines	American Airlines is a US-based airline and also the largest airline in the world in terms of total passengers-miles transported and fleet size, and the second-largest airline in the world in terms of total operating revenues. In the wake of the TWA merger, it began losing money. It underwent additional cost-cutting measures, including rolling back its "More Room Throughout Coach" program, ending three-class service on many international flights, and standardizing its fleet at each hub . However, the airline has rebounded and expanded its service into new markets, including Ireland, India and mainland China.
Cardinal health	Cardinal Health is a holding company.
Contract	A contract is a "promise" or an "agreement" that is enforced or recognized by the law. In the civil law, a contract is considered to be part of the general law of obligations.
Manpower	Manpower is an Employment Business and Agency established by Elmer Winter. Manpower has several subsidiaries including Elan, Jefferson Wells and Right Management. Manpower supplies staff to multinational corparations such as IBM, Monsanto, ntl and Danaher subsidiaries.
Department of	The Department of Defense is the federal department charged with coordinating and

106

Go to **Cram101.com** for the Practice Tests for this Chapter.

Defense	supervising all agencies and functions of the government relating directly to national security and the military.
International Paper	International Paper is an American pulp and paper company, the second largest pulp and paper company in the world. It was the largest producer of plastic lids and cups, manufacturing for the fast-food giants McDonalds, Wendys, and Subway.
Radio-frequency identification	Radio-frequency identification is an automatic identification method, relying on storing and remotely retrieving data using devices.
Wal-Mart	Wal-Mart is an American public corporation, currently the world's 2nd largest corporation according to the 2007 Fortune 500. It was founded by Sam Walton in 1962.
Erin Anderson	Erin Anderson was the John H. Loudon Chaired Professor of International Management and Professor of Marketing at INSEAD, France, which she became a part of in 1994. Her research was mostly focused on issues regarding the motivation, structuring, and control of the sales force and channels of distribution.
George S. Day	George S. Day is the Professor of Marketing at the Wharton School of Business, Pennsylvania, USA. His primary areas of activity are marketing, the management of new product development, strategic planning, organizational change and competitive strategies in global markets.
Research	Research is a human activity based on intellectual investigation and aimed at discovering, interpreting, and revising human knowledge on different aspects of the world. Research can use the scientific method, but need not do so.
Jan B. Heide	Jan B. Heide is the Irwin Maier Chair of Marketing at the UW-Madison School of Business. His areas of expertise include distribution channels, inter-organizational relationships, strategic decision-making, and vertical market restrictions. He received his Ph.D. from UW-Madison.

108

Go to **Cram101.com** for the Practice Tests for this Chapter.

Charrette	Charrette is one of the largest independent providers of imaging products to the graphics, corporate and technical design marketplaces in the United States. The company was founded in 1964 and has 22 offices throughout the country. Their products range from large-format
Customer	Customer is someone who makes use of or receives the products or services of an individual or organization.
Customer relationship management	Customer relationship management is a term applied to processes implemented by a company to handle their contact with their customers. Customer relationship management software is used to support these processes, storing information on customers and prospective customers.
Management	Management comprises directing and controlling a group of one or more people or entities for the purpose of coordinating and harmonizing that group towards accomplishing a goal. Management often encompasses the deployment and manipulation of human resources, financial resources, technological resources, and natural resources.
Relationship management	Relationship management is a broad term that covers concepts used by companies to manage their relationships with customers, including the capture, storage and analysis of customer, vendor, partner, and internal process information.
Integrated marketing	Integrated marketing is a planning process designed to assure that all brand contacts received by a customer or prospect for a product, service, or organization are relevant to that person and consistent over time. It is a combination of two or more forms of marketing used to sell a product or service
Marketing	Marketing is the process or act of bringing together buyers and sellers. Two major factors of marketing are the recruitment of new customers and the retention and expansion of relationships with existing customers. Marketing methods are informed by many of the social sciences, particularly psychology, sociology, and economics.
Marketing communication	A Marketing communication is a message and related media used to communicate with a market. Those who practice advertising, branding, direct marketing, graphic design, marketing, packaging, promotion, publicity, sponsorship, public relations, sales, sales promotion and online marketing are termed marketing communicators or marketing communication managers.
Meeting	In a meeting, two or more people come together for the purpose of discussing a usually predetermined topic such as business or community event planning, often in a formal setting.
Goal	An objective or goal is a personal or organizational desired end point in development. It is usually endeavored to be reached in finite time by setting deadlines.
Goal setting	In business, goal setting has the advantages of encouraging participants to put in substantial effort; and, because every member is aware of what is expected of him or her, little room is left for inadequate effort going unnoticed.
Planning	Planning is both the organizational process of creating and maintaining a plan; and the psychological process of thinking about the activities required to create a desired future on some scale.
Setting	Setting is one of the key factors for salespeople who are conducting sales presentations. The setting that the salesperson chooses should reflect the nature of the presentation.
Hierarchy of Effects Model	The Hierarchy of Effects Model is a method used in advertising which makes the presumption that a consumer must pass through a sequence of steps from initial awareness to eventual action. These stages include awareness, interest, evaluation, trial, and adoption.
Dow Corning	Dow Corning is a multinational corporation specialized in silicon and silicone-based technology, offering more than 7,000 products and services. A large, majority-owned subsidiary of Dow Corning Corporation is the Hemlock Semiconductor Corporation. Class-action lawsuits claimed that it's silicone breast implants caused systemic health problems. The

claims first centered around breast cancer, and then migrated to a range of autoimmune

Brand	A brand includes a name, logo, slogan, and/or design scheme associated with a product or service. Brand recognition and other reactions are created by the use of the product or service and through the influence of advertising, design, and media commentary. A brand is a symbolic embodiment of all the information connected to the product and serves to create associations and expectations around it.
DuPont	DuPont is an American chemical company that is currently the world's second largest chemical company in terms of market capitalization and fourth in revenue.
Du Pont family	The Du Pont family is an American family descended from Pierre Samuel du Pont de Nemours. The son of a Paris watchmaker and a member of a Burgundian noble family, he and his sons, Victor Marie du Pont and Eleuthère Irénée du Pont, emigrated to the United States in 1800 and used the resources of this heritage to found one of the most prominent of American families, and one of its most successful corporations, E. I. du Pont de Nemours and Company,
IBM	IBM is a multinational computer technology and consulting corporation. It manufactures and sells computer hardware, software, infrastructure services, hosting services and consulting services in areas ranging from mainframe computers to nanotechnology.
Positioning	The art and science of fitting the product or service to one or more segments of the market in such a way as to set it meaningfully apart from competition is called positioning.
Prospects	Prospects are potential customers, clients, or buyers of goods and services; the act of searching for a prospect.
Strategic goal	A strategic goal is a broad statement of where an organization wants to be in the future; pertains to the organization as a whole rather than to specific divisions or departments.
Tactical goals	Goals that define the outcomes that major divisions and departments must achieve in order for the organization to reach its overall goals are referred to as tactical goals.
Dow Chemical	The Dow Chemical is an American multinational corporation. It is currently the second largest chemical manufacturer in the World and major provider of plastics, chemicals, and agricultural products. Dow Chemical holds itself to be one of the top world companies in innovation and research and development, with more than $1 billion annual expenditure in R&D and the single largest concentration of PhD's and Engineers in the United States.
Intel	Intel is the world's largest semiconductor company and the inventor of the x86 series of microprocessors, the processors found in many personal computers. After 2000, growth in demand for high-end microprocessors slowed and competitors garnered significant market share, initially in low-end and mid-range processors but ultimately across the product range, and it's dominant position was reduced. Intel has become one of the world's most recognizable computer brands following its long-running "Intel Inside" campaign.
Goal-setting theory	Goal-setting theory is one of the most popular theories in organizational psychology. It attempts to affect performance by implementing actions to achieve a desired prospect.
Hewlett-Packard	Hewlett-Packard is currently the world's largest information technology corporation and is known worldwide for its printers, personal computers and high end servers. The company, which once catered primarily to engineering and medical markets—a line of business it spun off as Agilent Technologies in 1999 now markets to households and small business. It is acknowledged by Wired magazine as the producer of the world's first personal computer, in 1968, the Hewlett-Packard 9100A.
YouTube	YouTube is a video sharing website where users can upload, view and share video clips. YouTube was created in mid-February 2005 by three former PayPal employees. The San Bruno-based service uses Adobe Flash technology to display a wide variety of user-generated video

Go to **Cram101.com** for the Practice Tests for this Chapter.

	content, including movie clips, TV clips and music videos, as well as amateur content such as videoblogging and short original videos. In October 2006, Google Inc. announced that it had reached a deal to acquire the company for US$1.65 billion in Google stock. The deal closed on November 13, 2006.
Trade	A mechanism that allows trade is called a market. The original form of trade was barter, the direct exchange of goods and services. Modern traders instead generally negotiate through a medium of exchange, such as money.
Trade journal	A trade journal is a periodical, magazine or publication printed with the intention of target marketing to a specific industry or type of trade/business. A trade journal typically contains heavy advertising content focused on the industry in question with little if any "general audience" advertising.
Advertising	Advertising refers to paid, nonpersonal communication through various media by organizations and individuals who are in some way identified in the advertising message.
Internet	In business, the internet is viewed as an essential marketing tool for the advertisement of products and services, as well as a very valuable source of maintaining customer contact and communication.
Search engine	A search engine is an information retrieval system designed to help find information stored on a computer system. A Search engine helps in the minimization of the time required to find information and the amount of information which must be consulted, akin to other techniques for managing information overload.
Search engine marketing	In Internet marketing, search engine marketing is a set of marketing methods to increase the visibility of a website in search engine results pages.
Sugging	Sugging is a market research industry term, meaning "selling under the guise of research". This behavior occurs when a product marketer falsely pretends to be a market researcher conducting a survey, when in reality they are simply trying to sell the product in question.
Public relations	Public Relations is the managing of outside communication of an organization or business to create and maintain a positive image. It involves popularizing successes, downplaying failures, announcing changes, and many other activities.
Telemarketing	Telemarketing is a method of direct marketing in which a salesperson uses the telephone to solicit prospective customers to buy products or services. Telemarketing can also include recorded sales pitches programmed to be played over the phone via automatic dialing.
Sales	Sales is the act of providing a product or service in return for money or other compensation. It is an act of completion of a commercial activity.
Trade show	A trade show is an exhibition organized so tha companies in a specific industry can showcase and demostrate their new products and services. It often involve a considerable marketing investment by participating companies. Costs include space rental, display design and construction, telecommunications and networking, travel, accommodations, promotional literature, and "give away" items.
Belgacom	The Belgacom Group, composed of Belgacom NV/SA and its subsidiaries, is the leading telecommunications company in Belgium.
Message	A message in its most general meaning is an object of communication.
Touchpoint	A touchpoint is all of the physical, communication and human interactions audiences experience over their relationship with an organization.
Marketing research	Marketing Research is a form of business research and is generally divided into two categories: consumer market research and business-to-business market research, which was

previously known as Industrial Marketing Research.

Research	Research is a human activity based on intellectual investigation and aimed at discovering, interpreting, and revising human knowledge on different aspects of the world. Research can use the scientific method, but need not do so.
Arthur Andersen	Arthur Andersen was once one of the Big Five accounting firms, performing auditing, tax, and consulting services for large corporations. In 2002 the firm voluntarily surrendered its licenses to practice as Certified Public Accountants in the U.S. pending the result of prosecution by the U.S. Department of Justice over the firm's handling of the auditing of Enron.
Buyer	A buyer is any person who contracts to acquire an asset in return for some form of consideration.
Coca-Cola	Coca-Cola is the world's most recognizable brand, according to BusinessWeek. The first serving in 1886 cost US$0.05. The Coca-Cola is the world's largest consumer of natural vanilla extract. The exact formula of Coca-Cola is a famous trade secret. The original copy of the formula is held in SunTrust Bank's main vault in Atlanta.
Disney	The Walt Disney Company is the second largest media and entertainment corporation in the world, after Time Warner, according to Forbes. Founded on October 16, 1923 by brothers Walt and Roy Disney as a small animation studio, it has become one of the biggest Hollywood studios, and owner of eleven theme parks and several television networks, including the American Broadcasting Company.
Kraft	Kraft Foods Inc. is the second-largest food and beverage company headquartered in North America behind PepsiCo and the third largest in the world after Nestlé SA and PepsiCo.
Lee	Lee is a brand of denim jeans founded in Salina, Kansas, headquartered in Kansas City, Kansas, U.S.A., and owned by the VF Corporation. Lee didn't become an important factor in its industry until when it conceived the Union-All.
Leo Burnett	Leo Burnett was an advertising executive famous for creating such icons as the Jolly Green Giant, the Marlboro Man, Toucan Sam, Charlie the Tuna, Morris the Cat, the Pillsbury Doughboy, the 7up "Spot", and Tony the Tiger.
Nike	Nike is a major American supplier of athletic shoes, apparel and sports equipment. It's marketing strategy is an important component of the company's success. Nike is positioned as a premium-brand, selling well-designed and expensive products. Nike had no direct competitors because there was no single brand which could compete directly with Nike's range of sports and non-sports oriented gear until Reebok came along in the 1980s.
Sara Lee	Sara Lee is a global consumer-goods company based in Downers Grove, Illinois, USA. Sara Lee announced a new company wide campaign: "the joy of eating." The campaign is part of a restructuring at Sara Lee, that has shown Sara Lee focus its efforts on its core Food & Beverage brands, including its namesake Fresh Bakery, Deli and Sweet Goods Brands.
Strategy	A strategy is a long term plan of action designed to achieve a particular goal, most often "winning". Strategy is differentiated from tactics or immediate actions with resources at hand by its nature of being extensively premeditated, and often practically rehearsed.
Cyrix	Cyrix was a CPU manufacturer that began in 1988 in Richardson, TX as a specialist supplier of high-performance math co-processors for 286 and 386 systems. The company was founded by former Texas Instruments staff members and had a long but troubled relationship with TI throughout its history.
Motorola	Motorola is an American multinational communications company based in Schaumburg, Illinois, a Chicago suburb. Motorola developed the first truly global communication network using a set

Go to **Cram101.com** for the Practice Tests for this Chapter.

of 66 satellites. The business ambitions behind this project and the need for raising venture capital to fund the project led to the creation of the Iridium company. Recently, it has ventured off to start a wireless phone service with Bradford Mobile Phones, and Kansas City Gold.

Acquisition	An acquisition, is the buying of one company by another. An acquisition may be friendly or hostile. In the former case, the companies cooperate in negotiations; in the latter case, the acquisition target is unwilling to be bought or the target's board has no prior knowledge of the offer. Acquisition usually refers to a purchase of a smaller firm by a larger one.
Customer acquisition	Customer Acquisition is a term used to describe the methodologies and systems to manage customer prospects and inquiries, generally generated by a variety of marketing techniques. It can be considered the connectivity between advertising and customer relationship management.
Larry Ellison	Larry Ellison is the billionaire co-founder and CEO of Oracle Corporation, a major database software company.
Benefits	Employee benefits are various non-wage compensations provided to employees in addition to their normal wages or salaries. Where an employee exchanges cash wages for some other form of benefit, this is generally referred to as a 'salary sacrifice' arrangement. In most countries, most kinds of employee benefits are taxable to at least some degree.
Budget	Budget generally refers to a list of all planned expenses and revenues. A budget is an important concept in microeconomics, which uses a budget line to illustrate the trade-offs between two or more goods. In other terms, a budget is an organizational plan stated in monetary terms.
DHL	DHL is a Deutsche Post World Net company of Germany that provides international Mail, Express, Logistics and Finance. The company was founded in 1969 by Adrian Dalsey, Larry Hillblom, and Robert Lynn.
Objective-and-task budgeting	An advertising budget method in which advertising expenditures are determined on the basis of a specific audit of the resources needed to achieve the specific objectives and tasks outlined in the advertiser's media plan is a objective-and-task budgeting.
Cynthia Rodriguez Cano	Dr. Cynthia Rodriguez Cano is an Assistant Professor of Marketing at Georgia College and State University. She earned her Ph.D. in marketing from University of South Florida in Tampa, Florida. Her academic research has appeared respected publications such as the International Journal of Research in Marketing and the Journal of Personal Selling & Sales Management.

Bendix	Bendix was founded in 1924 in South Bend, Indiana, United States, by the inventor Vincent Bendix. At first it manufactured brake systems for cars and trucks. It supplied General Motors with braking systems for its production lines for several decades. In 1929 Vincent
Customer	Customer is someone who makes use of or receives the products or services of an individual or organization.
Lifetime value	In marketing, lifetime value is the present value of the future cash flows attributed to the customer relationship. Use of lifetime value as a marketing metric tends to place greater emphasis on customer service and long-term customer satisfaction, rather than on maximizing short-term sales.
Leadership	Some commentators link leadership closely with the idea of management. Some regard the two as synonymous, and others consider management a subset of leadership. This would allow for a reciprocal relationship between leadership and management, implying that an effective manager should possess leadership skills, and an effective leader should demonstrate management skills.
Value	Value of a product within the context of marketing means the relationship between the consumer's expectations of product quality to the actual amount paid for it. It can be defined by both qualitative and quantitative measures. On the qualitative side, value is the perceived gain composed of individual's emotional, mental and physical condition plus various social, economic, cultural and environmental factors. On the quantitative side, value is the actual gain measured in terms of financial numbers, percentages, and dollars.
Bruce Adams	Bruce Adams is the founder and owner of the Bruce L. Adams Company, an enterprise that restores classic 190 SL Mercedes-Benz automobiles to the specifications of the original manufacturer for its clients. He presently serves as Newsletter Editor for the International 190 SL Group and is a member of their Board of Directors. He is also a member of the Tri-Angle Section of the Mercedes-Benz Club of America, as well as the editor of their newsletter.
NASCAR	Nascar is the largest sanctioning body of motorsports in the United States. The three largest racing series sanctioned by it are the NEXTEL Cup, the Busch Series and the Craftsman Truck Series. Tobacco companies, which had been banned from television advertising, found a popular and demographically suitable consumer base in Nascar fans and engaged it as a promotional outlet.
Advertising	Advertising refers to paid, nonpersonal communication through various media by organizations and individuals who are in some way identified in the advertising message.
Attitude	Attitude is a hypothetical construct that represents an individual's like or dislike for an item. Attitudes are positive, negative or neutral views of an "attitude object": i.e. a person, behavior or event. People can also be "ambivalent" towards a target, meaning that they simultaneously possess a positive and a negative bias towards the attitude in question.
Awareness	In biological psychology, awareness comprises a human's or an animal's perception and cognitive reaction to a condition or event. It may also refer to public or common knowledge or understanding about a social, scientific, or political issue, and hence many movements try to foster "awareness" of a given subject.
Marketing	Marketing is the process or act of bringing together buyers and sellers. Two major factors of marketing are the recruitment of new customers and the retention and expansion of relationships with existing customers. Marketing methods are informed by many of the social sciences, particularly psychology, sociology, and economics.
Media	In communication, media are the storage and transmission tools used to store and deliver information or data. It is often referred to as synonymous with mass media or news media, but

	may refer to a single medium used to communicate any data for any purpose.
Media plan	A document consisting of objectives, strategies, and tactics for reaching a target audience through various media vehicles is a media plan.
Goal setting	In business, goal setting has the advantages of encouraging participants to put in substantial effort; and, because every member is aware of what is expected of him or her, little room is left for inadequate effort going unnoticed.
Plan	Informal or ad-hoc plan are created by individuals in all of their pursuits. Structured and formal plans, used by multiple people, are more likely to occur in projects, diplomacy, careers, economic development, military campaigns, combat, or in the conduct of other business.
United Van Lines	United Van Lines is a moving van company now part of UniGroup, Inc. It is the largest mover in the United States with more than 30% market share. United offers free, professional in-home estimates and moving tips to assist consumers with the moving process.
Airline	An airline provides air transport services for passengers or freight, generally with a recognized operating certificate or license. An Airline will lease or own their aircraft with which to supply these services and may form partnerships or alliances with other airline companies for mutual benefit.
American Airlines	American Airlines is a US-based airline and also the largest airline in the world in terms of total passengers-miles transported and fleet size, and the second-largest airline in the world in terms of total operating revenues. In the wake of the TWA merger, it began losing money. It underwent additional cost-cutting measures, including rolling back its "More Room Throughout Coach" program, ending three-class service on many international flights, and standardizing its fleet at each hub . However, the airline has rebounded and expanded its service into new markets, including Ireland, India and mainland China.
BASF	BASF AG is a German chemical company and the largest chemical company in the world. BASF has customers in over 200 countries and supplies products to a wide variety of industries. Despite its size and global presence BASF receives little public attention as it has abandoned consumer product lines in the 90s.
IBM	IBM is a multinational computer technology and consulting corporation. It manufactures and sells computer hardware, software, infrastructure services, hosting services and consulting services in areas ranging from mainframe computers to nanotechnology.
Intel	Intel is the world's largest semiconductor company and the inventor of the x86 series of microprocessors, the processors found in many personal computers. After 2000, growth in demand for high-end microprocessors slowed and competitors garnered significant market share, initially in low-end and mid-range processors but ultimately across the product range, and it's dominant position was reduced. Intel has become one of the world's most recognizable computer brands following its long-running "Intel Inside" campaign.
Magazine	A magazine is a publication, generally published on a regular schedule, containing a variety of articles, generally financed by advertising, by a purchase price, or both.
Media selection	Media selection is the process of choosing the most cost-effective media to achieve the necessary coverage, and number of exposures, among the target audience.
Selection	Under selection, individuals with advantageous or "adaptive" traits tend to be more successful than their peers reproductively--meaning they contribute more offspring to the succeeding generation than others do.
Reed Elsevier	Reed Elsevier is a global publisher and information provider. It came into being in autumn 1992 as the result of a merger between Reed International, a British trade book and magazine

Go to **Cram101.com** for the Practice Tests for this Chapter.

publisher, and the Dutch science publisher Elsevier NV, forming the Reed Elsevier group, a dual-listed company consisting of Reed Elsevier PLC and Reed Elsevier NV. It is listed on several of the world's major stock exchanges.

Cost	In economics, business, and accounting, a cost is the value of money that has been used up to produce something.
Cost per mille	Cost per mille is a commonly used measurement in advertising. Radio, television, newspaper, magazine and online advertising can be purchased on the basis of what it costs to show the ad to one thousand viewers. It is used in marketing as a benchmark to calculate the relative cost of an advertising campaign or an ad message in a given medium.
Exhibit	Exhibit refers to a copy of a written instrument on which a pleading is founded, annexed to the pleading and by reference made a part of it. Any paper or thing offered in evidence and marked for identification.
Publishing	Publishing is the process of production and dissemination of literature or information – the activity of making information available for public view.
Reach	In the application of statistics to advertising and media analysis, reach is defined as the size of the audience who listen to, read, view or otherwise access a particular work in a given period.
Audit	An audit is an evaluation of a person, organization, system, process, project or product. An audit is performed to ascertain the validity and reliability of information, and also provide an assessment of a system's internal control. In financial accounting, an audit is an independent assessment of the fairness by which a company's financial statements are presented by its management.
Control system	A control system is a device or set of devices to manage, command, direct or regulate the behavior of other devices or systems. The term "control system" may be applied to the essentially manual controls that allow an operator to, for example, close and open a hydraulic press, where the logic requires that it cannot be moved unless safety guards are in place.
System	System is a set of interacting or interdependent entities, real or abstract, forming an integrated whole.
Canon	Canon is a Japanese company that specializes in imaging and optical products, including cameras, photocopiers and computer printers. Despite the company's high profile in the consumer market for cameras and computer printers, most of the company revenue comes from the office products division.
Dallas Convention Center	The Dallas Convention Center is a meeting hall, event/convention center and civic center in the Convention Center District of downtown Dallas, Texas.
Radio	Radio is the transmission of signals, by modulation of electromagnetic waves with frequencies below those of visible light. This can be detected and transformed into sound or other signals that carry information.
Southwest Airlines	Southwest Airlines is a low-fare airline in the United States. It is the largest airline in the United States by number of passengers carried domestically for any one year and the second largest airline in the world by number of passengers carried. Southwest Airlines is one of the world's most profitable airlines and in January 2007, posted a profit for the 34th consecutive year. Its reputation for low prices and a laid-back atmosphere have made it an icon of pop culture.
Television	Television is a widely used telecommunication system for broadcasting and receiving moving

Go to **Cram101.com** for the Practice Tests for this Chapter.

pictures and sound over a distance.

Exchange	The trade of things of value between buyer and seller so that each is better off after the trade is called the exchange.
International Business	International business is a term used to collectively describe topics relating to the operations of firms with interests in several countries. One of the results on the increasing success of International Business ventures is Globalization.
Lycos	Lycos is a search engine and web portal centered around broadband entertainment content. It began as a search engine research project by Dr. Michael Loren Mauldin of Carnegie Mellon University. It merged with Terra Networks of Spain, creating one of the world's largest Internet companies. Under new ownership, it began to refocus its strategy, moving away from a search-centric portal, toward a community destination for broadband entertainment content.
Yahoo	Yahoo is an American public corporation and global internet services company. Yahoo Search Marketing provides services such as Sponsored Search, Local Advertizing, and Product/Travel/Directory Submit that let different businesses advertise their products and services in the Yahoo network. Other forms of advertizing which bring in revenue for Yahoo include display and contextual advertizing.
Index	In economics and finance, an index is a single number calculated from an array of prices or of quantities. Examples are a price index, a quantity index, a market performance Index. Values of the index in successive periods summarize level of the activity over time or across economic units.
News	News is any new information or information on current events which is presented by print, broadcast, Internet, or word of mouth to a third party or mass audience.
Public relations	Public Relations is the managing of outside communication of an organization or business to create and maintain a positive image. It involves popularizing successes, downplaying failures, announcing changes, and many other activities.
Performance measurement	Performance measurement is the use of statistical evidence to determine progress toward specific defined organizational objectives.
Performance	A performance generally comprises an event in which one group of people behave in a particular way for another group of people.
Publicity	From a marketing perspective, publicity is one component of promotion. The other elements of the promotional mix are advertizing, sales promotion, and personal selling. It is primarily an informative activity, but its ultimate goal is to promote the client's products, services, or brands.
Press kit	A press kit is a pre-packaged set of promotional materials of a person, company, or organization distributed to members of the media for promotional use. They are often distributed to announce a release or for a news conference.
News release	A publicity tool consisting of an announcement regarding changes in the company or the product line is called a news release.
Press release	A written public news announcement normally distributed to major news services is referred to as press release.
Teradata	Teradata is a hardware and software vendor specializing in data warehousing and analytic technologies. It was formerly a division of NCR Corporation, the largest company in Dayton, Ohio. Their headquarters remain in Dayton. The spinoff from NCR occurred on October 1, 2007.
Lobbying	Lobbying is a concerted effort designed to achieve some result, typically from government authorities and elected officials. It can consist of the outreach of legislative members,

Go to **Cram101.com** for the Practice Tests for this Chapter.

public actions, or combinations of both public and private actions.

Trade
A mechanism that allows trade is called a market. The original form of trade was barter, the direct exchange of goods and services. Modern traders instead generally negotiate through a medium of exchange, such as money.

Trade show
A trade show is an exhibition organized so tha companies in a specific industry can showcase and demostrate their new products and services. It often involve a considerable marketing investment by participating companies. Costs include space rental, display design and construction, telecommunications and networking, travel, accommodations, promotional literature, and "give away" items.

Medical Imaging
Medical imaging refers to the techniques and processes used to create images of the human body for clinical purposes or medical science.

Service
In economics and marketing, a service is the non-material equivalent of a good. Service has been defined as an economic activity that does not result in ownership, and this is what differentiates it from providing physical goods.

Goal
An objective or goal is a personal or organizational desired end point in development. It is usually endeavored to be reached in finite time by setting deadlines.

CeBIT
CeBIT is the world's largest computer expo. It is held each spring on the world's largest fairground in Hanover, Germany, and is a barometer of the state of the art in information technology. With an exhibition area of roughly 450,000 m² and up to 700,000 visitors, it is larger than COMPUTEX and the no-longer held COMDEX.

Contract
A contract is a "promise" or an "agreement" that is enforced or recognized by the law. In the civil law, a contract is considered to be part of the general law of obligations.

Department of Defense
The Department of Defense is the federal department charged with coordinating and supervising all agencies and functions of the government relating directly to national security and the military.

Promotion
Promotion is one of the four key aspects of the marketing mix. The other three elements are product management, pricing, and distribution. Promotion involves disseminating information about a product, product line, brand, or company.

Alcatel
Alcatel-Lucent is a French company that provides hardware, software, and services to telecommunications service providers and enterprises all over the globe.

Attention
In advertising research, attention is the direct measure of a commercial's ability to win in the street fight for audience attention. It is one of the three report card measures attention, brand linkage and motivation.

Human resources
Human Resources refers to the individuals within the firm, and to the portion of the firm's organization that deals with hiring, firing, training, and other personel issues.

Strategy
A strategy is a long term plan of action designed to achieve a particular goal, most often "winning". Strategy is differentiated from tactics or immediate actions with resources at hand by its nature of being extensively premeditated, and often practically rehearsed.

Dallas Cowboys
The Dallas Cowboys are a professional American football team in the Eastern Division of the National Football Conference in the National Football League. They are based in the Dallas suburb of Irving, Texas. The team currently plays their home games at Texas Stadium in Irving, but they are scheduled to move to a new stadium in nearby Arlington in 2009.

Roger Staubach
Roger Staubach is a businessmanand legendary Hall of Fame quarterback for the Dallas Cowboys from 1969 until 1979. The Staubach Company, which has been his primary endeavor since retirement from football, and where he served as its Chairman and Chief Executive Officer. He

Go to **Cram101.com** for the Practice Tests for this Chapter.

Chapter 11. Communicating via Advertising, Trade Shows, and PR

	founded an eponymous commercial real estate brokerage firm headquartered in Dallas, Texas.
Technology	Technology is a broad concept that deals with a species' usage and knowledge of tools and crafts, and how it affects a species' ability to control and adapt to its environment. In human society, it is a consequence of science and engineering, although several technological advances predate the two concepts.
Texas Ranger Division	The Texas Ranger Division is a law enforcement agency with statewide jurisdiction based in Austin, the capital of Texas, in the United States.
Attraction efficiency	In relation to internet marketing, attraction efficiency refers to the attractiveness at converting an aware person into a "hit" at a website. In other words, it is the measured efficiency of the combination of the language and images utilized to attract new customers. The attraction efficiency of a website is the ratio number of hits to the number of aware surfers.
Event sponsorship	A type of promotion whereby a company develops sponsorship relations with a particular event such as a concert, sporting event, or other activity is referred to as event sponsorship.
Specialty advertising	An advertising, sales promotion, and motivational communications medium that employs useful articles of merchandise imprinted with an advertiser's name, message, or logo is referred to as specialty advertising.
Split premium	A split premium is a mortgage plan that combines an up-front premium with monthly premiums. The up-front premium is due at the closing of a sale, whereas the monthly premium is billed by the seller beginning with the month that the first payment is due from the borrower.
Efficiency	Efficiency is a general term for the value assigned to a situation by some measure designed to reduce the amount of waste or "friction" or other undesirable economic features present.
Premium	Premium refers to the fee charged by an insurance company for an insurance policy. The rate of losses must be relatively predictable: In order to set the premium (prices) insurers must be able to estimate them accurately.
Sponsor	To sponsor something is to support an event, activity, person, or organization financially or through the provision of products or services. A sponsor is the individual or group that provides the support, similar to a benefactor.
Software	Software is a general term used to describe a collection of computer programs, procedures and documentation that perform some task on a computer system.
Corporation	A corporation is a legal entity which has a separate legal personality from its members. The defining legal rights and obligations of the corporation are: the ability to sue and be sued; the ability to hold assets in its own name; the ability to hire agents; the ability to sign contracts; and the ability to make by-laws, which govern its internal affairs.
Radio-frequency identification	Radio-frequency identification is an automatic identification method, relying on storing and remotely retrieving data using devices.
Russell Abratt	Russell Abratt is the Associate Dean of Internal Affairs and a Professor of Marketing at the Huizenga School at Nova Southeastern University, Ft. Lauderdale. He was Director of Academic Programmes and the FNB Professor of Marketing at the Graduate School of Business Administration, University of the Witwatersrand, Johannesburg. He holds a B.com, MBA and a Ph.D, in Business Administration. Before he became involved with the academic world, Abratt worked in Operations Management for Foschini and in Marketing Management for Frank and Hirsch, the South African distributors of Citizen, Aiwa, Nikon and Polaroid amongst others.
Poul Houman Andersen	Dr. Poul Houman Andersen is the Profesor of Management at the Aarhus School of Business.

130

Go to **Cram101.com** for the Practice Tests for this Chapter.

Les Carlson	Dr. Les Carlson is a Professor of Marketing at the College of Business and Behavioral Science. His research interests include consumer socialization, environmental advertising, memory measurement, the differential effect of advertising on children and parents; and the explanations for consumerism, diffusion of innovations and cognitive processing of advertising.

Go to **Cram101.com** for the Practice Tests for this Chapter.

Direct marketing	Direct marketing is a sub-discipline and type of marketing. There are two main definitional characteristics which distinguish it from other types of marketing or advertising. The first is that it attempts to send its messages directly to consumers, without the use of
Marketing	Marketing is the process or act of bringing together buyers and sellers. Two major factors of marketing are the recruitment of new customers and the retention and expansion of relationships with existing customers. Marketing methods are informed by many of the social sciences, particularly psychology, sociology, and economics.
InfoUsa	infoUSA is a provider of both business and consumer information and marketing solutions, which consists of data processing, database management and email marketing. infoUSA is a publicly traded company since 1992 on the NASDAQ stock exchange under the ticker symbol IUSA. infoUSA has over 4 million customers worldwide and revenues in 2006 were over $700 million.
CDW	CDW, headquartered in Vernon Hills, Illinois, is a leading reseller of computer hardware, software and supplies. Along with its warehouse-attached showroom in Illinois, CDW takes orders from its catalog via mail order, telephone and the Internet.
Compiled list	Compiled list is a list of people or businesses from telephone and business directories that have not necessarily responded to any offers. It is used in an entire market and offers a good way to select a high percent of particular types of business.
Information	Information is the result of processing, gathering, manipulating and organizing data in a way that adds to the knowledge of the receiver. In other words, it is the context in which data is taken.
Media	In communication, media are the storage and transmission tools used to store and deliver information or data. It is often referred to as synonymous with mass media or news media, but may refer to a single medium used to communicate any data for any purpose.
Publishing	Publishing is the process of production and dissemination of literature or information – the activity of making information available for public view.
Telequalifying	Telequalifying is a method of selling that focuses on account research, account mapping, interest development, and preliminary analysis to determine whether or not the prospect "qualifies" to be within the customer demographic. It is a form of customer analysis that is focused on qualifying inquires and/or generating leads through vigorous outbound calling efforts.
Renting	Renting is an agreement where a payment is made for the temporary use of a good or property owned by another person or company.
American Express	American Express is a diversified global financial services company. American Express became one of the monopolies that President Theodore Roosevelt had the Interstate Commerce Commission investigate during his administration. American Express acquired the investment banking and trading firm, Lehman Brothers Kuhn Loeb, and added it to the Shearson family, creating Shearson Lehman/American Express.
Magazine	A magazine is a publication, generally published on a regular schedule, containing a variety of articles, generally financed by advertising, by a purchase price, or both.
Goal	An objective or goal is a personal or organizational desired end point in development. It is usually endeavored to be reached in finite time by setting deadlines.
Distribution	Distribution is one of the 4 aspects of marketing. Traditionally, distribution has been seen as dealing with logistics: how to get the product or service to the customer. There have also been some innovations in the distribution of services. For example, there has been an increase in franchizing and in rental services - the latter offering anything from televisions through tools.

Go to **Cram101.com** for the Practice Tests for this Chapter.

Direct orders	The result of direct marketing offers that contain all the information necessary for a prospective buyer to make a decision to purchase and complete the transaction are direct orders.
Sales	Sales is the act of providing a product or service in return for money or other compensation. It is an act of completion of a commercial activity.
Superior benefit	A superior benefit is the tactic of mentioning a benefit that may outweigh the customer's specific concern in a product or service.
Strategy	A strategy is a long term plan of action designed to achieve a particular goal, most often "winning". Strategy is differentiated from tactics or immediate actions with resources at hand by its nature of being extensively premeditated, and often practically rehearsed.
Federal Express	Federal Express is a cargo airline, printing, and courier company offering overnight courier, ground, heavy freight, document copying and logistics services.
Tyson	Tyson is an American multinational corporation based in Springdale, Arkansas, that operates in the food industry. The company is the world's largest processor and marketer of chicken, beef, and pork, and annually exports the largest percentage of beef out of the United States.
Telemarketing	Telemarketing is a method of direct marketing in which a salesperson uses the telephone to solicit prospective customers to buy products or services. Telemarketing can also include recorded sales pitches programmed to be played over the phone via automatic dialing.
Shell	Shell is a multinational oil company of British and Dutch origins. It is one of the largest private sector energy corporations in the world, and one of the six "supermajors".
Account	In accountancy, an account is a label used for recording and reporting a quantity of almost anything. Most often it is a record of an amount of money owned or owed by or to a particular person or entity, or allocated to a particular purpose.
Management	Management comprises directing and controlling a group of one or more people or entities for the purpose of coordinating and harmonizing that group towards accomplishing a goal. Management often encompasses the deployment and manipulation of human resources, financial resources, technological resources, and natural resources.
Dormant	Dormant is a state lacking activity; it can refer to several things including a company that is currently inactive.
Dormant account	A dormant account is a member account that has had no deposit or withdrawal activity for a certain period of time.
In-house	In-house refers to the production of some commodity or service, such as a television program, using a company's own funds, staff, or resources.
Service	In economics and marketing, a service is the non-material equivalent of a good. Service has been defined as an economic activity that does not result in ownership, and this is what differentiates it from providing physical goods.
Email	Email is a store and forward method of composing, sending, storing, and receiving messages over electronic communication systems.
SPAM	SPAM luncheon meat is a canned precooked meat product made by the Hormel Foods Corporation. The labelled ingredients in the Classic variety of Spam are: chopped pork shoulder meat with ham meat added, salt, water, sugar, and sodium nitrite to help "keep its color".
Effectiveness	Effectiveness means the capability of producing an effect.
Tonka	Tonka is an American toy company most known for its signature toy trucks and construction equipment.

Synergy	Synergy refers to the phenomenon in which two or more discrete influences or agents acting together create an effect greater than that predicted by knowing only the separate effects of the individual agents.
Website	A website is a collection of Web pages, images, videos or other digital assets that is hosted on one or several Web server, usually accessible via the Internet, cell phone or a LAN.
Online transaction processing	Online transaction processing, or OLTP, refers to a class of systems that facilitate and manage transaction-oriented applications, typically for data entry and retrieval transaction processing. The term is somewhat ambiguous; some understand a "transaction" in the context of computer or database transactions, while others define it in terms of business or commercial transactions. OLTP has also been used to refer to processing in which the system responds immediately to user requests. An automatic teller machine for a bank is an example of a commercial transaction processing application.
Web robot	A web robot is a software applications that run automated tasks over the Internet. It typically performs tasks that are both simple and structurally repetitive, at a much higher rate than would be possible for a human editor alone. It is also being used as organization and content access applications for media delivery.
Cisco	Cisco designs and sells networking and communications technology and services under five brands, namely Cisco, Linksys, WebEx, IronPort, and Scientific Atlanta. Initially, Cisco manufactured only enterprise multi-protocol routers but gradually diversified its product offering to move into the home user market with the purchase of Linksys while also expanding its offering for corporate customers.
Corporation	A corporation is a legal entity which has a separate legal personality from its members. The defining legal rights and obligations of the corporation are: the ability to sue and be sued; the ability to hold assets in its own name; the ability to hire agents; the ability to sign contracts; and the ability to make by-laws, which govern its internal affairs.
Dell	Dell develops, manufactures, sells and supports personal computers, servers, data storage devices, network switches, personal digital assistants, software, televisions, computer peripherals and other technology-related products.
Software	Software is a general term used to describe a collection of computer programs, procedures and documentation that perform some task on a computer system.
Hotel	A hotel is an establishment that provides paid lodging, usually on a short-term basis. It often provides a number of additional guest services such as a restaurant, a swimming pool or childcare. Some establishments have conference services and meeting rooms and encourage groups to hold conventions and meetings at their location.
Steve Spangler	Steve Spangler is an author, professional speaker, Emmy Award winner, listed in the Time 100, science teacher, founder of two companies, toy maker and a trained magician. He is most famous for the hugely popular experiment of dropping a Mentos into a bottle of Diet Coke, with the end result being a huge geyser of Diet Coke.
Integrated marketing	Integrated marketing is a planning process designed to assure that all brand contacts received by a customer or prospect for a product, service, or organization are relevant to that person and consistent over time. It is a combination of two or more forms of marketing used to sell a product or service
Marketing communication	A Marketing communication is a message and related media used to communicate with a market. Those who practice advertising, branding, direct marketing, graphic design, marketing, packaging, promotion, publicity, sponsorship, public relations, sales, sales promotion and online marketing are termed marketing communicators or marketing communication managers.
Dave Allen	Dave Allen is a Sheffield based businessman and ex-chairman of football team Sheffield

	Wednesday. Allen owns a 99.9% share of the A & S Leisure Group which runs Napoleons Casinos across England, as well as the greyhound racing track at Owlerton Stadium in Sheffield.
Avnet	Avnet, Inc. is a technology B 2 B distributor headquartered in Phoenix, Arizona. Avnet, Inc., is one of the world's largest value-added distributors of semiconductors, connectors, passive and electromechanical components, and RF & microwave devices; enterprise networking and computer equipment, and embedded subsystems from leading manufacturers. Serving customers in 70 countries, Avnet markets, inventories, and adds value to these products.
Columbus College of Art and Design	Columbus College of Art and Design is a private college of art and design located in downtown Columbus, Ohio. Originally founded in 1879 as The Columbus Art School, CCAD is one of the oldest operating art schools in the United States. Located in the central portion of Columbus, the college consists of ten acres and 16 buildings and is adjacent to the Columbus Museum of Art and Columbus State Community College. Approximately 1,300 full-time students enroll at CCAD every academic year.
Design	Design, usually considered in the context of the applied arts, engineering, architecture, and other such creative endeavors, is used both as a noun and a verb. As a verb, "to design" refers to the process of originating and developing a plan for a product, structure, system, or component.

Hewlett-Packard	Hewlett-Packard is currently the world's largest information technology corporation and is known worldwide for its printers, personal computers and high end servers. The company, which once catered primarily to engineering and medical markets—a line of business it spun off as
Mark Hurd	Mark Hurd is the chairman, chief executive officer, and president of Hewlett-Packard. He previously spent 25 years at NCR Corporation, culminating in his two-year tenure as chief executive officer and president. His leadership was marked by successful efforts to improve operating efficiency, bolster the position of NCR's product line and build a strong leadership team.
Sales	Sales is the act of providing a product or service in return for money or other compensation. It is an act of completion of a commercial activity.
Google	Google is an American public corporation, specializing in Internet search and online advertising. It's mission statement is, "to organize the world's information and make it universally accessible and useful." While the company's primary business interest is in the web content arena, Google has begun experimenting with other markets, such as radio and print publications. Most of it's revenue is derived from advertising programs.
IBM	IBM is a multinational computer technology and consulting corporation. It manufactures and sells computer hardware, software, infrastructure services, hosting services and consulting services in areas ranging from mainframe computers to nanotechnology.
Lee	Lee is a brand of denim jeans founded in Salina, Kansas, headquartered in Kansas City, Kansas, U.S.A., and owned by the VF Corporation. Lee didn't become an important factor in its industry until when it conceived the Union-All.
Microsoft	Microsoft is an American multinational computer technology corporation. develops, manufactures, licenses and supports a wide range of software products for computing devices. Microsoft has footholds in other markets besides operating systems and office suites, with assets such as the MSNBC cable television network, the MSN Internet portal, and the Microsoft Encarta multimedia encyclopedia. It has often been described as having a developer-centric business culture.
ServiceMaster	ServiceMaster a Fortune 500 company that provides various services to residences and firms. Its movement into business services makes it a large outsourcing company. Executive Vice President Steven C. Preston was appointed Administrator of the Small Business Administration.
Staples	Staples is the world's largest office supply retail store chain, with over 1,700 stores worldwide. Staples and Office Depot announced plans to merge. The Federal Trade Commission decided that the superpower would unfairly increase office supply prices despite competition from the third-in-line, which did not have stores in many of the local markets that the merger would affect.
Manpower	Manpower is an Employment Business and Agency established by Elmer Winter. Manpower has several subsidiaries including Elan, Jefferson Wells and Right Management. Manpower supplies staff to multinational corparations such as IBM, Monsanto, ntl and Danaher subsidiaries.
Behavior	Behavior refers to the actions or reactions of an object or organism, usually in relation to the environment. Behavior can be conscious or unconscious, overt or covert, and voluntary or involuntary. In animals, behavior is controlled by the endocrine system and the nervous system.
Business ethics	Business ethics is a form of the art of applied ethics that examines ethical principles and moral or ethical problems that can arise in a business environment.
Sales manager	A Sales manager implements various sales strategies and management techniques in order to facilitate improved profits and increased sales volume. They are also responsible for coordinating the sales and marketing department as well as over site concerning the fair and

honest execution of the sales process by his agents.

Value
Value of a product within the context of marketing means the relationship between the consumer's expectations of product quality to the actual amount paid for it. It can be defined by both qualitative and quantitative measures. On the qualitative side, value is the perceived gain composed of individual's emotional, mental and physical condition plus various social, economic, cultural and environmental factors. On the quantitative side, value is the actual gain measured in terms of financial numbers, percentages, and dollars.

Management
Management comprises directing and controlling a group of one or more people or entities for the purpose of coordinating and harmonizing that group towards accomplishing a goal. Management often encompasses the deployment and manipulation of human resources, financial resources, technological resources, and natural resources.

Organization
An organization is a social arrangement which pursues collective goals, which controls its own performance, and which has a boundary separating it from its environment.

Relationship management
Relationship management is a broad term that covers concepts used by companies to manage their relationships with customers, including the capture, storage and analysis of customer, vendor, partner, and internal process information.

Role
A role is a set of connected behaviors, rights and obligations as conceptualized by actors in a social situation. It is mostly defined as an expected behavior in a given individual social status and social position.

Corporation
A corporation is a legal entity which has a separate legal personality from its members. The defining legal rights and obligations of the corporation are: the ability to sue and be sued; the ability to hold assets in its own name; the ability to hire agents; the ability to sign contracts; and the ability to make by-laws, which govern its internal affairs.

Dialogue
A dialogue is a reciprocal conversation between two or more entities.

Information
Information is the result of processing, gathering, manipulating and organizing data in a way that adds to the knowledge of the receiver. In other words, it is the context in which data is taken.

Deere and Company
Deere and Company is an American corporation based in Moline, Illinois, and the leading manufacturer of agricultural machinery in the world. It currently stands at 98th rank in Fortune 500 ranking. Deere and Company agricultural products, usually sold under the John Deere name, include tractors, combine harvesters, balers, planters/seeders, ATVs and forestry equipment. The company is also a leading supplier of construction equipment, as well as equipment used in lawn, grounds and turf care, such as ride-on lawn mowers, string trimmers, chainsaws, snowthrowers and for a short period, snowmobiles.

Ford
Ford is an American company that manufactures and sells automobiles worldwide. Ford introduced methods for large-scale manufacturing of cars, and large-scale management of an industrial workforce, especially elaborately engineered manufacturing sequences typified by the moving assembly lines.

Industry
Industry, is the segment of economy concerned with production of goods. Industry began in its present form during the 1800s, aided by technological advances, and it has continued to develop to this day.

Strategy
A strategy is a long term plan of action designed to achieve a particular goal, most often "winning". Strategy is differentiated from tactics or immediate actions with resources at hand by its nature of being extensively premeditated, and often practically rehearsed.

Canon
Canon is a Japanese company that specializes in imaging and optical products, including cameras, photocopiers and computer printers. Despite the company's high profile in the

consumer market for cameras and computer printers, most of the company revenue comes from the office products division.

Consultative selling	Consultative selling emphasizes customer needs and meeting those needs with solutions combining products and/or services. A salesperson typically provides detailed instruction or advice on which solution best meets these needs.
Partnership	A partnership is a type of business entity in which partners share with each other the profits or losses of the business undertaking in which all have invested.
Delivery	Delivery is the process of transporting goods. Most goods are delivered through a transportation network. Cargo is primarily delivered via roads and railroads on land, shipping lanes on the sea and airline networks in the air. Certain specialized goods may be delivered via other networks, such as pipelines for liquid goods, power grids for electrical power and computer networks such as the Internet or broadcast networks for electronic information.
Expectation	In the case of uncertainty, expectation is what is considered the most likely to happen. An expectation, which is a belief that is centred on the future, may or may not be realistic.
Commitment	Personal commitment is the act or quality of voluntarily taking on or fulfilling obligations. What makes personal commitment "personal" is the voluntary aspect. In particular, it is not necessary that a personal commitment relate to personal interests.
Monitoring	Monitoring competence can be described as awareness of what you know.
Setting	Setting is one of the key factors for salespeople who are conducting sales presentations. The setting that the salesperson chooses should reflect the nature of the presentation.
Customer	Customer is someone who makes use of or receives the products or services of an individual or organization.
Customer service	Customer service is the provision of service to customers before, during and after a purchase. Its importance varies by product, industry and customer. As an example, an expert customer might require less pre-purchase service than a novice. In many cases, customer service is more important if the purchase relates to a "service" as opposed to a "product".
General Mills	General Mills is a corporation, mainly concerned with food products, which is headquartered in Golden Valley, Minnesota, a suburb of Minneapolis. The company markets such brands as Betty Crocker, Progresso, Yoplait, Old El Paso, and Pillsbury, as well as numerous well-known breakfast cereals. General Mills often uses product placement on Millsberry.
Upgrade	The term upgrade is most often used in computing and consumer electronics, generally meaning a replacement of hardware, software or firmware with a newer version, in order to bring the system up to date. The word is also used by audiophiles to describe the replacement of a product with a better quality product with the aim of bringing enhancements to sound quality.
Up-selling	Up-selling is a sales technique whereby a salesman attempts to have the customer purchase more expensive items, upgrades, or other add-ons in an attempt to make a more profitable sale. Up-selling usually involves marketing more profitable services or products, but up-selling can also be simply exposing the customer to other options he or she may not have considered previously. Up-selling can imply selling something additional, or selling something that is more profitable or otherwise preferable for the seller instead of the original sale.
Service	In economics and marketing, a service is the non-material equivalent of a good. Service has been defined as an economic activity that does not result in ownership, and this is what differentiates it from providing physical goods.
Training	Training refers to the acquisition of knowledge, skills, and competencies as a result of the

Go to **Cram101.com** for the Practice Tests for this Chapter.

teaching of vocational or practical skills and knowledge that relates to specific useful skills. It forms the core of apprenticeships and provides the backbone of content at technical colleges and polytechnics.

Cross-selling	Cross-selling is the term used to describe the sale of additional products or services to a customer. Less frequently it is used to describe the sale of services to additional business units at an account or to different geographic units of a customer.
Full-line selling	Full-line selling is the decision by a manufacturer to offer a large number of product variations in a particular product line.
Motorola	Motorola is an American multinational communications company based in Schaumburg, Illinois, a Chicago suburb. Motorola developed the first truly global communication network using a set of 66 satellites. The business ambitions behind this project and the need for raising venture capital to fund the project led to the creation of the Iridium company. Recently, it has ventured off to start a wireless phone service with Bradford Mobile Phones, and Kansas City Gold.
PPG Industries	PPG Industries is an American manufacturer of glass and chemical products, including automotive safety glass. It is also the world's third largest producer of chlorine and caustic soda, vinyl chloride, and chlorinated solvents. It recently made an offer to Bain Capital to buy the SigmaKalon Group of companies, which produce paints and speciality coating.
Status	Social status is the honor or prestige attached to one's position in society one's social position. The stratification system, which is the system of distributing rewards to the members of society, determines social status.
Supply chain	A supply chain, logistics network, or supply network is the system of organizations, people, activities, information and resources involved in moving a product or service from suppli-er to customer. Supply chain activities transform raw materials and components into a finished product that is delivered to the end customer.
Power	Much of the recent sociological debate on power revolves around the issue of the enabling nature of power.
Accenture	Accenture Ltd. is a global management consulting, technology services, and outsourcing company with its main business office in Chicago, Illinois. It is the largest consulting firm in the world and is one of the largest computer services and software companies on the Fortune Global 500 list.
Council of American Survey Research Organizations	The Council of American Survey Research Organizations is the trade association of survey research organizations, representing over 250 companies and research operations in the United States and abroad. Since 1975, The Council of American Survey Research Organization has grown from a membership of 15 research firms to an organization of over 200 firms.
Square D	Square D is an American manufacturer of equipment used to control and distribute electric power headquartered in Palatine, Illinois. They were purchased by the French company Schneider Electric and they continue to sell into the commercial, industrial, and residential markets.
Account	In accountancy, an account is a label used for recording and reporting a quantity of almost anything. Most often it is a record of an amount of money owned or owed by or to a particular person or entity, or allocated to a particular purpose.
American Express	American Express is a diversified global financial services company. American Express became one of the monopolies that President Theodore Roosevelt had the Interstate Commerce Commission investigate during his administration. American Express acquired the investment banking and trading firm, Lehman Brothers Kuhn Loeb, and added it to the Shearson family,

creating Shearson Lehman/American Express.

Key accounts	Key accounts are a wholesaler's or manufacturer's primary customer accounts which provide the majority of their overall revenue.
R. R. Donnelley	R. R. Donnelley provides print and related services. In the late 1980s, the division was spun off as its own company, Geosystems, which in turn became MapQuest and is now a subsidiary of Time Warner.
Xerox	Xerox Corporation is a global document management company, which manufactures and sells a range of color and black-and-white printers, multifunction systems, photo copiers, digital production printing presses, and related consulting services and supplies.
Multi-level marketing	Multi-level marketing is a business model that combines direct marketing with franchizing. Multi-level marketing businesses function by recruiting salespeople to sell a product and offer additional sales commissions based on the sales of people recruited into their downline, an organization of people that includes direct recruits, recruits' recruits, etc.
Team selling	Using an entire team of professionals in selling to and servicing major customers is referred to as team selling.
NCR Corporation	NCR Corporation is a technology company specializing in products for the retail and financial sectors. Its main products are point-of-sale terminals, automatic teller machines, check processing systems, barcode scanners, and business consumables.
Workload	The term workload can refer to a number of different yet related entities. While a precise definition of a workload is elusive, a commonly accepted definition is the hypothetical relationship between a group or individual human operator and task demands.
Outsourcing	Outsourcing refers to the delegation of non-core operations from internal production to an external entity specializing in the management of that operation. Outsourcing is utilizing experts from outside the entity to perform specific tasks that the entity once performed itself.
Activity quota	A quota that focuses on the activities in which sales representatives are supposed to engage is an activity quota. Examples include number of letters to potential accounts, number of product demonstrations, number of calls on new accounts, and number of submitted proposals.
Outcome	An outcome is a set of moves or strategies taken by the players, or their payoffs resulting from the actions or strategies taken by all players.
Compensation	Deferred compensation is an arrangement in which a portion of an employee's income is paid out at a date after which that income is actually earned. Examples of deferred compensation include pensions, retirement plans, and stock options. The primary benefit of most deferred compensation is the deferral of tax to the dates at which the employee actually receives the income.
Quota	Racial quota in employment and education are numerical requirements for hiring, promoting, admitting and/or graduating members of a particular racial group while discriminating other racial groups. These quotas may be determined by governmental authority and backed by governmental sanctions. When the total number of jobs or enrollment slots is fixed, this proportion may get translated to a specific number
Commission	The payment of commission as currency for services rendered or products sold is a common way to reward sales people.
Salary	A salary is a form of periodic payment from an employer to an employee, which is specified in an employment contract. It is contrasted with piece wages, where each job, hour or other unit is paid separately, rather than on a periodic basis.

Cargo	Cargo is a term used to denote goods or produce being transported generally for commercial gain, usually on a ship, plane, train, van or truck.
Duty	Duty is a term that conveys a sense of moral commitment to someone or something.
Plan	Informal or ad-hoc plan are created by individuals in all of their pursuits. Structured and formal plans, used by multiple people, are more likely to occur in projects, diplomacy, careers, economic development, military campaigns, combat, or in the conduct of other business.
Performance	A performance generally comprises an event in which one group of people behave in a particular way for another group of people.
Evaluation	Evaluation is the systematic determination of merit, worth, and significance of something or someone. Evaluation often is used to characterize and appraise subjects of interest in a wide range of human enterprises, including the Arts, business, computer science, criminal justice, engineering, foundations and non-profit organizations, government, health care, and other human services.
Conversion	Conversion refers to any distinct act of dominion wrongfully exerted over another's personal property in denial of or inconsistent with his rights therein. That tort committed by a person who deals with chattels not belonging to him in a manner that is inconsistent with the ownership of the lawful owner.
Conversion ratio	Conversion ratio refers to the number of shares of common stock an investor will receive if he or she exchanges a convertible bond or convertible preferred stock for common stock.
Exhibit	Exhibit refers to a copy of a written instrument on which a pleading is founded, annexed to the pleading and by reference made a part of it. Any paper or thing offered in evidence and marked for identification.
Measurement	Measurement is the estimation of the magnitude of some attribute of an object, such as its length or weight, relative to a unit of measurement.
Good	A good in economics is any object or service that increases utility, directly or indirectly, not to be confused with good in a moral or ethical sense. A good that cannot be used by consumers directly, such as an office building or capital equipment, can also be referred to as a good as an indirect source of utility through resale value or as a source of income.
Christian Homburg	Christian Homburg is a Professor of Business Administration at the University of Mannheim in Germany. He received his Diploma in Mathematics and Business Administration from the University of Karlsruhe and a doctorate in Business Administration also from the University of Karlsruhe.
Stock	In financial terminology, stock is the capital raized by a corporation, through the issuance and sale of shares.

152

Go to **Cram101.com** for the Practice Tests for this Chapter.

DuPont	DuPont is an American chemical company that is currently the world's second largest chemical company in terms of market capitalization and fourth in revenue.
Du Pont family	The Du Pont family is an American family descended from Pierre Samuel du Pont de Nemours. The son of a Paris watchmaker and a member of a Burgundian noble family, he and his sons, Victor Marie du Pont and Eleuthère Irénée du Pont, emigrated to the United States in 1800 and
Agency	Agency is an area of commercial law dealing with a contractual or quasi-contractual tripartite set of relationships when an Agent is authorized to act on behalf of another called the Principal to create a legal relationship with a Third Party. Succinctly, it may be referred to as the relationship between a principal and an agent whereby the principal, expressly or impliedly, authorizes the agent to work under his control and on his behalf. The
Environmental Protection Agency	An administrative agency created by Congress in 1970 to coordinate the implementation and enforcement of the federal environmental protection laws is referred to as the Environmental Protection Agency.
Price	In economics and business, the price is the assigned numerical monetary value of a good, service or asset. Price typically is marked up by the percentage of choice by the seller to be able to make a profit from his cost or expenditure to create the product.
Corporation	A corporation is a legal entity which has a separate legal personality from its members. The defining legal rights and obligations of the corporation are: the ability to sue and be sued; the ability to hold assets in its own name; the ability to hire agents; the ability to sign contracts; and the ability to make by-laws, which govern its internal affairs.
NCR Corporation	NCR Corporation is a technology company specializing in products for the retail and financial sectors. Its main products are point-of-sale terminals, automatic teller machines, check processing systems, barcode scanners, and business consumables.
Demand	The demand represents the amount of a good that buyers are willing and able to purchase at various prices, assuming all other non-price factors remain the same. The demand curve is almost always represented as downwards-sloping, meaning that as price decreases, consumers will buy more of the good.
Supply	The supply is the relationship between the quantity of goods supplied by the producers of a good and the current market price. It is graphically represented by the supply curve. It is commonly represented as directly proportional to price.
Supply and demand	Supply and demand describe market relations between prospective sellers and buyers of a good. The supply and demand model determines price and quantity sold in the market. The model is fundamental in microeconomic analysis of buyers and sellers and of their interactions in a market. It is also used as a point of departure for other economic models and theories.
Inelastic	Inelastic refers to having an elasticity less than one. For a price elasticity of demand, this means that expenditure falls as price falls. For an income elasticity, it means that expenditure share falls with income.
Competitiveness	Competitiveness is a comparative concept of the ability and performance of a firm, sub-sector or country to sell and supply goods and/or services in a given market. The term may also be applied to markets, where it is used to refer to the extent to which the market structure may be regarded as perfectly competitive.
Competitive market	A market in which no buyer or seller has market power is called a competitive market.
Market	A market is, as defined in economics, a social arrangement that allows buyers and sellers to discover information and carry out a voluntary exchange of goods or services.
Learning	Learning is the acquisition and development of memories and behaviors, including skills,

	knowledge, understanding, values, and wisdom. It is the goal of education, and the product of experience.
Learning curve	The learning curve refers to a relationship between the duration of learning or experience and the resulting progress.
E. Jerome McCarthy	E. Jerome McCarthy is a professor at Michigan State University, USA, and an internationally known marketing consultant. He is one of the authors of the influential book "Basic Marketing".
Monopolistic competition	Monopolistic competition is a common market form. Many markets can be considered as monopolistically competitive, often including the markets for restaurants, cereal, clothing, shoes and service industries in large cities.
Competition	Competition is a rivalry between individuals, groups, or nations for territory or resources. It arises whenever two or more parties strive for a goal that cannot be shared. Competition occurs naturally between living organisms which coexist in the same environment. For example, animals compete over water supplies, food, and mates. In addition, humans compete for attention, wealth, prestige, and fame.
Quantity	Quantity is a kind of property which exists as magnitude or multitude.
Timothy Aeppel	Timothy Aeppel is the Staff Reporter for the Wall Street Journal. His articles are typically about the various changes within the business sector and how those changes affect the economy. Some of his articles have included topics such as the rising price of gas and the decreased number of jobs that pay a living wage, the Firestone Company's tire recall, and rising costs within the health care industry.
Pricing	Pricing is the manual or automatic process of applying prices to purchase and sales orders, based on factors such as: a fixed amount, quantity break, promotion or sales campaign, specific vendor quote, price prevailing on entry, shipment or invoice date, combination of multiple orders or lines, and many others.
Profit	Profit generally is the making of gain in business activity for the benefit of the owners of the business. The word comes from Latin meaning "to make progress", is defined in two different ways, one for economics and one for accounting.
Strategy	A strategy is a long term plan of action designed to achieve a particular goal, most often "winning". Strategy is differentiated from tactics or immediate actions with resources at hand by its nature of being extensively premeditated, and often practically rehearsed.
Distribution	Distribution is one of the 4 aspects of marketing. Traditionally, distribution has been seen as dealing with logistics: how to get the product or service to the customer. There have also been some innovations in the distribution of services. For example, there has been an increase in franchizing and in rental services - the latter offering anything from televisions through tools.
Margin	In finance, a margin is collateral that the holder of a position in securities, options, or futures contracts has to deposit to cover the credit risk of his counterparty.
Monsanto	Monsanto is a multinational agricultural biotechnology corporation. It is the world's leading producer of the herbicide glyphosate, marketed as "Roundup". The company is also by far the leading producer of genetically engineered seed.
Management	Management comprises directing and controlling a group of one or more people or entities for the purpose of coordinating and harmonizing that group towards accomplishing a goal. Management often encompasses the deployment and manipulation of human resources, financial resources, technological resources, and natural resources.
Customer	Customer is someone who makes use of or receives the products or services of an individual or

organization.

Territorial restriction	A territorial restriction typically consists of a promise made by a dealer that he or she will sell the purchased goods from a manufacturer neither outside an area specified by the manufacturer nor to customers who reside or have their place of business outside that determined area. This practice is utilized in order to strengthen the position of the supplier and the franchise.
Advertising	Advertising refers to paid, nonpersonal communication through various media by organizations and individuals who are in some way identified in the advertising message.
Hewlett-Packard	Hewlett-Packard is currently the world's largest information technology corporation and is known worldwide for its printers, personal computers and high end servers. The company, which once catered primarily to engineering and medical markets—a line of business it spun off as Agilent Technologies in 1999 now markets to households and small business. It is acknowledged by Wired magazine as the producer of the world's first personal computer, in 1968, the Hewlett-Packard 9100A.
Push/pull relationship	The push/pull relationship is that between a product or piece of information and who is moving it. A customer "pulls" things towards themselves, while a producer "pushes" things toward customers.
Product line	A group of products that are physically similar or are intended for a similar market are called the product line.
Product line pricing	The setting of prices for all items in a product line is called product line pricing.
Complementary products	Products that use similar technologies and can coexist in a family of products are called complementary products. They tend to be purchased jointly and whose demands therefore are related.
Substitute product	Any product viewed by a consumer as an alternative for other products is a substitute product. The substitution is rarely perfect, and varies from time to time depending on price, availability, etc.
Price discrimination	Price discrimination exists when sales of identical goods or services are transacted at different prices from the same provider. In a theoretical market with perfect information, no transaction costs and a prohibition on secondary exchange to prevent arbitrage, price discrimination can only be a feature of monopoly markets.
Robinson-Patman Act	The Robinson-Patman Act is a United States federal law that prohibits anticompetitive practices by producers, specifically price discrimination. It grew out of practices in which chain stores were allowed to purchase goods at lower prices than other retailers. The Act provided for criminal penalties, but contained a specific exemption for "cooperative associations".
Market segment	A Market segment is a subgroup of people or organizations sharing one or more characteristics that cause them to have similar product needs.
Discrimination	Discrimination comes from the Latin discriminare, which means to "distinguish between". However, it is more than distinction or differentiation; it is action based on prejudice resulting in unfair treatment of other people.
Administered price	A price for a good or service that is set and maintained by government, usually requiring accompanying restrictions on trade if the administered price differs from the world price.
Bid	A bid is the highest price that a buyer is willing to pay for a good.
Department of	The Department of Energy is a Cabinet-level department of the United States government

Energy	responsible for energy policy and nuclear safety. Its purview includes the nation's nuclear weapons program, nuclear reactor production for the United States Navy, energy conservation, energy-related research, radioactive waste disposal, and domestic energy production.
Discount	The difference between the face value of a bond and its selling price, when a bond is sold for less than its face value it's referred to as a discount.
Discounts and allowances	Discounts and allowances are reductions to a basic price. They could modify either the manufacturer's list price, the retail price, or the list price.
Trade discount	Trade discount is a payments to distribution channel members for performing some function . Examples of these functions are warehousing and shelf stocking. It is most frequent in industries where retailers hold the majority of the power in the distribution channel.
PPG Industries	PPG Industries is an American manufacturer of glass and chemical products, including automotive safety glass. It is also the world's third largest producer of chlorine and caustic soda, vinyl chloride, and chlorinated solvents. It recently made an offer to Bain Capital to buy the SigmaKalon Group of companies, which produce paints and speciality coating.
Decision	A decision is a final product of a specific mental/cognitive process by an individual or group, which is called decision making, or in more detail, Inactive decision making, Reactive decision making, and Proactive decision making. Therefore it is a subjective concept. It is a mental object and can be an opinion, a rule or a task for execution/application.
Decision theory	Decision theory is an interdisciplinary area of study, related to and of interest to practitioners in all branches of science, engineering and in all human social activities. It is concerned with how real or ideal decision-makers make or should make decisions, and with how optimal decisions can be reached.
Department of Defense	The Department of Defense is the federal department charged with coordinating and supervising all agencies and functions of the government relating directly to national security and the military.
Bidding	Bidding is an offer of setting a price one is willing to pay for something. A price offer is called a bid. The term may be used in context of auctions, stock exchange or card games.
Auction	An auction is the process of buying and selling goods by offering them up for bid, taking bids, and then selling the item to the winning bidder. In economic theory, an auction is a method for determining the value of a commodity that has an undetermined or variable price.
Negotiation	Negotiation is the process whereby interested parties resolve disputes, agree upon courses of action, bargain for individual or collective advantage, and/or attempt to craft outcomes which serve their mutual interests.
Andean Group	Andean Group is a trade organization in Lima, Peru. In 1969, Bolivia, Chile, Colombia, Ecuador, and Peru established the group by the Treaty of Cartagena. In 1973, Venezuela joined. Chile quit in 1976, as did Peru in 1992. The group created a free trade area called the Andean Pact in 1992.
Avoidance	Avoidance is a controversial method of dealing with conflict which attempts to avoid directly confronting the issue at hand. Methods of doing this can include changing the subject, putting off a discussion until later, or simply not bringing up the subject of contention
Collaboration	Collaboration occurs when the interaction between groups is very important to goal attainment and the goals are compatible. Wherein people work together —applying both to the work of individuals as well as larger collectives and societies.
Compromise	In arguments, compromise is a concept of finding agreement through communication, through a mutual acceptance of terms—often involving variations from an original goal or desire.

Go to **Cram101.com** for the Practice Tests for this Chapter.

European Union	The European Union is a sui generis supranational union, made up of twenty-seven member states. It was established as the European Economic Community in 1957 by the Treaty of Rome and has undergone many changes since, most notably in 1992 by the Maastricht Treaty. Since 1957 new accessions have raised the number of member states, and powers have expanded. As a result, the EU can be described as both a supranational and an intergovernmental body.
Service	In economics and marketing, a service is the non-material equivalent of a good. Service has been defined as an economic activity that does not result in ownership, and this is what differentiates it from providing physical goods.
Contract	A contract is a "promise" or an "agreement" that is enforced or recognized by the law. In the civil law, a contract is considered to be part of the general law of obligations.
Nucor	Nucor is one of the largest steel producers in the United States, and the largest of the "mini-mill" operators. Nucor claims to be the largest recycler of scrap steel in the United States, recycling over 19 million tons of scrap steel annually. The company initiated liquidation proceedings, with the goal of selling its few remaining assets and distributing the cash to creditors and shareholders.
Robert J. Stevens	Robert J. Stevens serves as Chairman, President and Chief Executive Officer of Lockheed Martin.
System	System is a set of interacting or interdependent entities, real or abstract, forming an integrated whole.
McKinsey & Company	McKinsey & Company is a privately owned management consulting firm that focuses on solving issues of concern to senior management in large corporations and organizations. It operates under a practice of "up or out," in which consultants must advance in their consulting careers within a time frame, or else are asked to leave the company.
Das Narayandas	Das Narayandas is the James J. Hill Professor of Business Administration at Harvard Business School. He is the current co-chair of HBS's Program for Leadership Development. His credentials include a Bachelor of Technology degree in Engineering from the Indian Institute of Technology, a Ph.D. in Management from Purdue University, and a Post-Graduate Diploma in Management from his studies at the Indian Institute of Management.
John A. Quelch	John A. Quelch is a business school academic, administrator, public servant, corporate director and consultant. He served as Chairman of the board of the Massachusetts Port Authority, as well as Honorary COnsul General for the Kingdom of Morocco for the New England region.
Paction	Paction is a web-based application that enables the buyer and seller to prepare, negotiate, and complete contracts for the international sale and purchase of goods. The application produces contracts that are based on the International Chamber of Commerce's model international sale contract, which provides a comprehensible and precise set of conditions that are intended to balance the interests of sellers and buyers.
Mark E. Bergen	Mark E. Bergen is the Carolyn I. Anderson Professor of Business Education Excellence and Chair of the Department of Marketing & Logistics Management at the Carlson School of Management. His main area of research focuses on pricing and channels of distribution, where he has studied issues such as pricing as a strategic capability, pricing wars, price pass-through, branded variants, dual distribution, gray markets, co-op advertising, and quick response.
Reed K. Holden	Reed K. Holden is an expert in pricing who uses his expertise in building valuable customers with business-to-business firms, financial and information services, technology and outsourcing, and medical device and distribution companies. He has advised companies on the differences in the go-to-market strategies that enhance price leadership and profitable

growth. Dr. Holden works with large corporations around the world to manage with an outside-in view of his customers. He advocates the utilization of the Value Discipline process and the need for companies to adapt their organization in highly competitive markets.

Lee
Lee is a brand of denim jeans founded in Salina, Kansas, headquartered in Kansas City, Kansas, U.S.A., and owned by the VF Corporation. Lee didn't become an important factor in its industry until when it conceived the Union-All.

Levy
Levy refers to imposing and collecting a tax or tariff.

Stock
In financial terminology, stock is the capital raized by a corporation, through the issuance and sale of shares.

Tektronix	Tektronix is a North American company best known for its test and measurement equipment such as oscilloscopes, logic analyzers, and video and mobile test protocol equipment. As of November 2007, Tektronix is a subsidiary of Danaher Corporation.
Customer	Customer is someone who makes use of or receives the products or services of an individual or organization.
Customer equity	Customer Equity is the Net Present Value of a customer from the perspective of a supplier. It can - and should - also include customer goodwill that is normally not expressed in financial terms.
Marketing	Marketing is the process or act of bringing together buyers and sellers. Two major factors of marketing are the recruitment of new customers and the retention and expansion of relationships with existing customers. Marketing methods are informed by many of the social sciences, particularly psychology, sociology, and economics.
Telindus	Telindus is a group of companies which offer ICT services and solutions to the corporate and public sector internationally. They also offer management and support services in relation to their ICT contracts. The company was founded by John Cordier in 1969.
Control system	A control system is a device or set of devices to manage, command, direct or regulate the behavior of other devices or systems. The term "control system" may be applied to the essentially manual controls that allow an operator to, for example, close and open a hydraulic press, where the logic requires that it cannot be moved unless safety guards are in place.
Equity	Equity is the name given to the set of legal principles, in countries following the English common law tradition, which supplement strict rules of law where their application would operate harshly, so as to achieve what is sometimes referred to as "natural justice."
System	System is a set of interacting or interdependent entities, real or abstract, forming an integrated whole.
Operational	Operational, in a process context, also can denote a working method or a philosophy that focuses principally on cause and effect relationships of specific interest to a particular domain at a particular point in time. As a working method, it does not consider issues related to a domain that are more general.
Toleration	Toleration is a term used in social, cultural and religious contexts to describe attitudes and practices that prohibit discrimination against those whose practices or group memberships may be disapproved of by those in the majority.
Input-output	Refers to the structure of intermediate transactions among industries, in which one industry's output is an input to another, or even to itself are input-output.
Macro-control	Macro-control refers to the use of direct government intervention by the central government of the People's Republic of China to cool down the overheated economy.
Analysis	Analysis means literally to break a complex problem down into smaller, more manageable "independent" parts for the purposes of examination — with the hope that solving these smaller parts will lead to a solution of the more complex problem as well.
IBM	IBM is a multinational computer technology and consulting corporation. It manufactures and sells computer hardware, software, infrastructure services, hosting services and consulting services in areas ranging from mainframe computers to nanotechnology.
Salesforce.com	Salesforce.com is an on-demand Customer Relationship Management solution vendor.
Cycle time	In business, cycle time is the total amount of time that has elapsed from the beginning to the end of the sales process, as defined by the vendor and the buyer. Cycle time includes

Go to **Cram101.com** for the Practice Tests for this Chapter.

process time, during which a unit is acted upon to bring it closer to an output, and delay time, where a unit of work is spent waiting to take further action.

Federal Express	Federal Express is a cargo airline, printing, and courier company offering overnight courier, ground, heavy freight, document copying and logistics services.
Efficiency	Efficiency is a general term for the value assigned to a situation by some measure designed to reduce the amount of waste or "friction" or other undesirable economic features present.
Automatic Data Processing Lightspeed	Automatic Data Processing Lightspeed is a software company that assists dealers and industry consultants in creating software that meets the requirements of dealerships.
Balanced Scorecard	Balanced scorecard, a concept for measuring a company's activities in terms of its vision and strategies, to give managers a comprehensive view of the performance of a business. The key new element is focusing not only on financial outcomes but also on the human issues that drive those outcomes, so that organizations focus on the future and act in their long-term best interest. The strategic management system forces managers to focus on the important performance metrics that drive success. It balances a financial perspective with customer, process, and employee perspectives. Measures are often indicators of future performance.
Variance	Variance refers to a measure of how much an economic or statistical variable varies across values or observations. Its calculation is the same as that of the covariance, being the covariance of the variable with itself.
Observation	Observation is either an activity of a living being, which senses and assimilates the knowledge of a phenomenon, or the recording of data using instruments.
Tinkering variance	Tinkering variance is the act of making changes within a process in order to make the process more productive. This may include the implementation of new software, new customer services techniques, or value-based offers that intend to ease previous tensions and discrepancies between buyers and sellers.
Distribution center	A distribution center for a set of products is a warehouse or other specialized building with refrigeration or air conditioning which is stocked with products to be re-distributed to retailers or wholesalers.
Selection and recruitment of salespeople	The selection and recruitment of salespeople is determined by the analysis of the potential employee's personality, skills, goals, and previous experience. This is perhaps one of the most important decisions an organization can make - as the manner in which salespeople represent themselves also reflects upon the prestige and accountability of the organization.
Association to Advance Collegiate Schools of Business	The Association to Advance Collegiate Schools of Business was founded in 1916 to accredit schools of business worldwide, while the first accreditations took place in 1919. The stated mission is to advance quality management education worldwide through accreditation and thought leadership.
Benchmarking	Benchmarking is a process used in management and particularly strategic management, in which organizations evaluate various aspects of their processes in relation to best practice, usually within their own sector. This then allows organizations to develop plans on how to adopt such best practice, usually with the aim of increasing some aspect of performance.
Distribution	Distribution is one of the 4 aspects of marketing. Traditionally, distribution has been seen as dealing with logistics: how to get the product or service to the customer. There have also been some innovations in the distribution of services. For example, there has been an increase in franchizing and in rental services - the latter offering anything from televisions through tools.

Channel conflict	Channel conflict occurs when manufacturers disintermediate their channel partners, such as distributors, retailers, dealers, and sales representatives, by selling their products direct to consumers through general marketing methods and/or over the internet through eCommerce. It can also occur when there has been over production. This results in a surplus of products in the market place.
Conoco	Conoco was an American oil company founded as the Continental Oil and Transportation Company. Based in Ogden, Utah, the company was a coal, oil, kerosene, grease and candles distributor in the West. Seagram Company Ltd. engineered a takeover of Conoco. Although Seagram acquired a 32.2% stake in Conoco, DuPont was brought in as a white knight by the oil company and entered the bidding war. In the end, Seagram lost out in the Conoco bidding war.
Management	Management comprises directing and controlling a group of one or more people or entities for the purpose of coordinating and harmonizing that group towards accomplishing a goal. Management often encompasses the deployment and manipulation of human resources, financial resources, technological resources, and natural resources.
Setting	Setting is one of the key factors for salespeople who are conducting sales presentations. The setting that the salesperson chooses should reflect the nature of the presentation.
Budget	Budget generally refers to a list of all planned expenses and revenues. A budget is an important concept in microeconomics, which uses a budget line to illustrate the trade-offs between two or more goods. In other terms, a budget is an organizational plan stated in monetary terms.
Engineering	Engineering is the applied science of acquiring and applying knowledge to design, analysis, and/or construction of works for practical purposes.
Pricing	Pricing is the manual or automatic process of applying prices to purchase and sales orders, based on factors such as: a fixed amount, quantity break, promotion or sales campaign, specific vendor quote, price prevailing on entry, shipment or invoice date, combination of multiple orders or lines, and many others.
Quota	Racial quota in employment and education are numerical requirements for hiring, promoting, admitting and/or graduating members of a particular racial group while discriminating other racial groups. These quotas may be determined by governmental authority and backed by governmental sanctions. When the total number of jobs or enrollment slots is fixed, this proportion may get translated to a specific number
Plan	Informal or ad-hoc plan are created by individuals in all of their pursuits. Structured and formal plans, used by multiple people, are more likely to occur in projects, diplomacy, careers, economic development, military campaigns, combat, or in the conduct of other business.
Sales	Sales is the act of providing a product or service in return for money or other compensation. It is an act of completion of a commercial activity.
Audit	An audit is an evaluation of a person, organization, system, process, project or product. An audit is performed to ascertain the validity and reliability of information, and also provide an assessment of a system's internal control. In financial accounting, an audit is an independent assessment of the fairness by which a company's financial statements are presented by its management.
Marketing audit	Marketing audit is a fundmental part of the marketing planning process. It is conducted by the beginning of the process bu also at a series of points during implementation of the plan. It considers the internal and external influences on maketing planning.
Measurement	Measurement is the estimation of the magnitude of some attribute of an object, such as its length or weight, relative to a unit of measurement.

Customer satisfaction	Customer satisfaction, a business term, is a measure of how products and services supplied by a company meet or surpass customer expectation. It is seen as a key performance indicator within business and is part of the four perspectives of a Balanced Scorecard.
Contribution	In business organization law, the cash or property contributed to a business by its owners is referred to as contribution.
Contribution margin analysis	Contribution margin analysis is a technique used in brand marketing and product management to help a company decide what product to add to its product portfolio.
Full cost accounting	Full cost accounting generally refers to the process of collecting and presenting information for each proposed alternative when a decision is necessary. Costs and advantages may be considered in terms of environmental, economical and social impacts. Full cost accounting information may be used by decision-makers.
Activity-based costing	Activity-based costing is a method of allocating costs to products and services. It is generally used as a tool for planning and control. This is a necessary tool for doing value chain analysis.
Bank	A bank is a financial institution that acts as a payment agent for customers, and borrows and lends money. In some countries such as Germany and Japan banks are the primary owners of industrial corporations while in other countries such as the United States banks are prohibited from owning non-financial companies.
Case analysis	Case analysis is one of the most general and applicable methods of analytical thinking, depending only on the division of a problem, decision or situation into a sufficient number of separate cases.
Information	Information is the result of processing, gathering, manipulating and organizing data in a way that adds to the knowledge of the receiver. In other words, it is the context in which data is taken.
Information systems	Information systems is the system of persons, data records and activities that process the data and information in a given organization, including manual processes or automated processes. The study of information systems, originated as a sub-discipline of computer science, in an attempt to understand and rationalize the management of technology within organizations. It has matured into a major field of management.
Royal Bank of Canada	The Royal Bank of Canada is Canada's largest company. It is the largest financial institution in Canada in both assets and market capitlization. It maintains a profitable base from its Caribbean operations, and has retained high brand recognition among its other top competitors.
Statistics	Statistics is a mathematical science pertaining to the collection, analysis, interpretation or explanation, and presentation of data. It is applicable to a wide variety of academic disciplines, from the natural and social sciences to the humanities. Statistics are also used for making informed decisions.
Experiment	In the scientific method, an experiment is a set of observations performed in the context of solving a particular problem or question, to support or falsify a hypothesis or research concerning phenomena. The experiment is a cornerstone in the empirical approach to acquiring deeper knowledge about the physical world.
Andrew V. Abela	Andrew V. Abela is the Assistant Professor of Marketing at The Catholic University of America's Department of Business and Economics. He is perhaps best known for his articles that he has written for the Action Institute, an organization dedicated to the study of religion and liberty and their application to business ethics. He has written numerous articles on topics such as the ethical questions raised by consummerism and on the pragmatic approach of sales presentations, favoring the evidence-based design.

Packaging	Packaging is the science, art and technology of enclosing or protecting products for distribution, storage, sale, and use. Packaging also refers to the process of design, evaluation, and production of packages.
LexisNexis	LexisNexis is a popular searchable archive of content from newspapers, magazines, legal documents and other printed sources. It claims to be the "world's largest collection of public records, unpublished opinions, forms, legal, news, and business information" while offering their products to a wide range of professionals in the legal, risk management, corporate, government, law enforcement, accounting and academic markets.
Observational learning	Observational learning is learning that occurs as a function of observing, retaining and replicating behavior observed in others.
Reengineering	Reengineering is the radical redesign of an organization's processes, especially its business processes. Rather than organizing a firm into functional specialties and looking at the tasks that each function performs, one should be looking at complete processes from materials acquisition, to production, to marketing and distribution.
Design	Design, usually considered in the context of the applied arts, engineering, architecture, and other such creative endeavors, is used both as a noun and a verb. As a verb, "to design" refers to the process of originating and developing a plan for a product, structure, system, or component.
Planning	Planning is both the organizational process of creating and maintaining a plan; and the psychological process of thinking about the activities required to create a desired future on some scale.
Strategic planning	The process of determining the major goals of the organization and the policies and strategies for obtaining and using resources to achieve those goals is called strategic planning. Strategic Planning is the formal consideration of an organization's future course.
Manufacturing	Manufacturing is the use of tools and labor to make things for use or sale. The term may refer to a vast range of human activity, from handicraft to high tech, but is most commonly applied to industrial production, in which raw materials are transformed into finished goods on a large scale.
Lerzan Aksoy	Lerzan Aksoy is Assistant Professor of Marketing at Koc University in Istanbul, Turkey. Her research focuses on consumer satisfaction and its relationship to the spending patterns of consumers, customer relationship management, the effects of recommendation agents in the online environment, and customer decision quality. She co-authored the book "Loyalty Myths" with Timothy L. Keningham, Terry G. Vavra and Henri Wallard, a 2005 Wiley publication.
Gregory S. Carpenter	Gregory S. Carpenter is a Professor of Marketing Strategy at the Kellogg Business School, providing instruction in masters, doctoral, and executive programs. Professor Carpenter was voted Outstanding Professor of the Year by the Kellogg Managers' Program in 1992, and received the Sidney J. Levy Teaching Award in 1996. He was recognized by the journal BusinessWeek as an outstanding faculty in its Guide to the Best Business Schools.
Pradeep K. Chintagunta	Pradeep K. Chintagunta is a professor of marketing at the University of Chicago Graduate School of Business who is known for his quantitative research on household purchasing patterns with the use of scanner panel data, investigation of competitive marketing strategies, and studies involving the entertainment industry.
Colgate	Colgate, an oral hygiene product line and one of the namesake brands of the Colgate-Palmolive Company, is a manufacturer of a wide range of toothpastes and toothbrushes.

Plumtree	Plumtree was founded on the premise that the technology used to build the World Wide Web could support new kinds of corporate applications: Internet protocols could not only connect browsers to servers, but connect servers to one another, integrating electronic resources
Epiphany	Epiphany, previously known as E.piphany and Epiphany Marketing Software, was a company developing Customer Relationship Management software. On September 29, 2005, Epiphany was acquired by SSA Global Technologies. Epiphany CRM software is now produced by Infor, which acquired SSA Global in 2006.
Ford	Ford is an American company that manufactures and sells automobiles worldwide. Ford introduced methods for large-scale manufacturing of cars, and large-scale management of an industrial workforce, especially elaborately engineered manufacturing sequences typified by the moving assembly lines.
Motorola	Motorola is an American multinational communications company based in Schaumburg, Illinois, a Chicago suburb. Motorola developed the first truly global communication network using a set of 66 satellites. The business ambitions behind this project and the need for raising venture capital to fund the project led to the creation of the Iridium company. Recently, it has ventured off to start a wireless phone service with Bradford Mobile Phones, and Kansas City
Alexander the Great	Alexander the Great was an ancient Greek king of Macedon. He was one of the most successful military commanders in history, and is presumed undefeated in battle. By the time of his death, he had conquered most of the world known to the ancient Greeks.
Always-a-share customers	Always-a-share customers are consumers that buy from a merchant with a lower average value or lower frequency than those customers who prefer to make purchases from a specific merchant. They are the consumers that make purchases from an array of different competitors in accordance to product needs and prices versus loyalty.
Customer	Customer is someone who makes use of or receives the products or services of an individual or organization.
Customer retention	Customer retention refers to the percentage of customers who return to a service provider or continue to purchase a manufactured product.
Lifetime value	In marketing, lifetime value is the present value of the future cash flows attributed to the customer relationship. Use of lifetime value as a marketing metric tends to place greater emphasis on customer service and long-term customer satisfaction, rather than on maximizing short-term sales.
Probability	Probability is the likelihood that something is the case or will happen. Probability theory is used extensively in areas such as statistics, mathematics, science and philosophy to draw conclusions about the likelihood of potential events and the underlying mechanics of complex systems.
Retention	In marketing & sales terminology : Sales retention is the department or the action needed to retain the current customers, subscribers.
Value	Value of a product within the context of marketing means the relationship between the consumer's expectations of product quality to the actual amount paid for it. It can be defined by both qualitative and quantitative measures. On the qualitative side, value is the perceived gain composed of individual's emotional, mental and physical condition plus various social, economic, cultural and environmental factors. On the quantitative side, value is the actual gain measured in terms of financial numbers, percentages, and dollars.
Customer relationship management	Customer relationship management is a term applied to processes implemented by a company to handle their contact with their customers. Customer relationship management software is used to support these processes, storing information on customers and prospective customers.

Go to **Cram101.com** for the Practice Tests for this Chapter.

Management	Management comprises directing and controlling a group of one or more people or entities for the purpose of coordinating and harmonizing that group towards accomplishing a goal. Management often encompasses the deployment and manipulation of human resources, financial resources, technological resources, and natural resources.
Relationship management	Relationship management is a broad term that covers concepts used by companies to manage their relationships with customers, including the capture, storage and analysis of customer, vendor, partner, and internal process information.
Performance	A performance generally comprises an event in which one group of people behave in a particular way for another group of people.
Social	Social refers to human society or its organization.
Interpersonal ties	In mathematical sociology, interpersonal ties are defined as information-carrying connections between people. Interpersonal ties, generally, come in three varieties: strong, weak, or absent.
Shelby D. Hunt	Shelby D. Hunt is the Jerry S. Rawls and P. W. Horn Professor of Marketing. He was previously an editor for the Journal of Marketing from 1984-1987, and a chairman of the Marketing Department at the University of Wisconsin-Madison from 1974-1980.
IBM	IBM is a multinational computer technology and consulting corporation. It manufactures and sells computer hardware, software, infrastructure services, hosting services and consulting services in areas ranging from mainframe computers to nanotechnology.
Modular design	In the context of systems engineering, modular design is an approach aiming to subdivide a system into smaller parts that can be independently created and then used in different systems to drive multiple functionalities.
System	System is a set of interacting or interdependent entities, real or abstract, forming an integrated whole.
Investment	Investment refers to spending for the production and accumulation of capital and additions to inventories. In a financial sense, buying an asset with the expectation of making a return.
Public relations	Public Relations is the managing of outside communication of an organization or business to create and maintain a positive image. It involves popularizing successes, downplaying failures, announcing changes, and many other activities.
Self-image	A person's self-image is the mental picture, generally of a kind that is quite resistant to change, that depicts not only details that are potentially available to objective investigation by others, but also items that have been learned by that person about himself or herself, either from personal experiences or by internalizing the judgments of others.
Department of Defense	The Department of Defense is the federal department charged with coordinating and supervising all agencies and functions of the government relating directly to national security and the military.
Drucker	Drucker as a business thinker took off in the 1940s, when his initial writings on politics and society won him access to the internal workings of General Motors, which was one of the largest companies in the world at that time. His experiences in Europe had left him fascinated with the problem of authority.
Starbucks	Starbucks is a dominant multinational coffeehouse chain based in the United States. Starbucks does not franchise with individuals within North America but does enter into licensing arrangements with some companies. It entered the music industry with the acquisition of Hear Music, and the film industry with the creation of Starbucks Entertainment. This feature will slowly be offered in limited markets.

Go to **Cram101.com** for the Practice Tests for this Chapter.

Customer satisfaction	Customer satisfaction, a business term, is a measure of how products and services supplied by a company meet or surpass customer expectation. It is seen as a key performance indicator within business and is part of the four perspectives of a Balanced Scorecard.
Measurement	Measurement is the estimation of the magnitude of some attribute of an object, such as its length or weight, relative to a unit of measurement.
Chrysler	Chrysler is an American automobile manufacturer. Chrysler is now the largest private automaker in North America. A joint venture with Mitsubishi called Diamond Star Motors strengthened the company's hand in the small car market. Chrysler acquired AMC primarily for its Jeep brand, although the failing Eagle Premier would be the basis for the Chrysler LH platform sedans. This bolstered the firm, although Chrysler was still the weakest of the Big Three.
Gateway	Gateway is an American computer hardware company which develops, manufactures, supports and markets a wide range of personal computers, computer monitors, servers, and computer accessories. Gateway directly and indirectly sells its products to third-party retailers, consumers, businesses, government agencies and educational institutions. The corporate structure and management of Gateway extends beyond the board of directors.
Microsoft	Microsoft is an American multinational computer technology corporation. develops, manufactures, licenses and supports a wide range of software products for computing devices. Microsoft has footholds in other markets besides operating systems and office suites, with assets such as the MSNBC cable television network, the MSN Internet portal, and the Microsoft Encarta multimedia encyclopedia. It has often been described as having a developer-centric business culture.
Cintas	Cintas operates more than 400 facilties throughout North America and provides highly specialized services to businesses, including the design and manufacturing of corporate identity uniform programs, entrance mats, restroom supplies, promotional products, first aid and safety products, fire protection services and document management services to approximately 800,000 businesses.
Federal Express	Federal Express is a cargo airline, printing, and courier company offering overnight courier, ground, heavy freight, document copying and logistics services.
Heinz	Heinz famous for both its "57 Varieties" slogan and its British commercial jingle "Beanz Meanz Heinz," is a processed food product company headquartered in Pittsburgh, Pennsylvania, in the United States of America.
Anticipation	In finance, anticipation is where debts are paid off early, generally in order to pay less interest.
Lagniappe	Lagniappe means a small gift given to a customer by a merchant at the time of a purchase, such as a 13th beignet when buying a dozen, or more broadly something given or obtained gratuitously or by way of good measure; a bonus.
Relevance	Relevance is a term used to describe how pertinent, connected, or applicable some information is to a given matter. It has unique significance in a variety of fields.
Leonard L. Berry	Dr. Leonard L. Berry is the Distinguished Professor of Marketing, and holds the M.B. Zale Chair in Retailing and Marketing Leadership in the Mays Business School at Texas A&M University. He is also Professor of Humanities in Medicine in the College of Medicine at The Texas A&M University System Health Science Center.
George S. Day	George S. Day is the Professor of Marketing at the Wharton School of Business, Pennsylvania, USA. His primary areas of activity are marketing, the management of new product development, strategic planning, organizational change and competitive strategies in global markets.

Go to **Cram101.com** for the Practice Tests for this Chapter.

Das Narayandas	Das Narayandas is the James J. Hill Professor of Business Administration at Harvard Business School. He is the current co-chair of HBS's Program for Leadership Development. His credentials include a Bachelor of Technology degree in Engineering from the Indian Institute of Technology, a Ph.D. in Management from Purdue University, and a Post-Graduate Diploma in Management from his studies at the Indian Institute of Management.
Valarie A. Zeithaml	Valarie A. Zeithaml is the David S. Van Pelt Family Distinguished Professor of Marketing at the Kenan-Flagler Business School. She is an internationally recognized pioneer of services marketing and has devoted 20 years to researching, consulting, and teaching service quality, customer equity, and services management.

Printed in the United States
144432LV00001B/67/P